Don't Know Much About®
Literature

Don't Know Much About® Literature

What you need to know but never learned about great books and authors

Kenneth C. Davis
& Jenny Davis

An Imprint of HarperCollins*Publishers*

DON'T KNOW MUCH ABOUT® LITERATURE. Copyright © 2009 by Kenneth C. Davis and Jenny Davis. All rights reserved. Printed in the United States of America. No part of this book may be used or reproduced in any manner whatsoever without written permission except in the case of brief quotations embodied in critical articles and reviews. For information address Harper-Collins Publishers, 10 East 53rd Street, New York, NY 10022.

HarperCollins books may be purchased for educational, business, or sales promotional use. For information please write: Special Markets Department, HarperCollins Publishers, 10 East 53rd Street, New York, NY 10022.

FIRST HARPERLUXE EDITION

HarperLuxe™ is a trademark of HarperCollins Publishers

Library of Congress Cataloging-in-Publication Data is available upon request.

ISBN: 978-0-06-177505-5

09 10 11 12 13 ID/RRD 10 9 8 7 6 5 4 3 2 1

This book is dedicated to
every child who ever asked "Why?"
And to every parent, teacher, librarian, friend,
and relative who might take the time to answer.

"Of making books, there is no end."

—ECCLESIASTES

"I cannot live without books."

—THOMAS JEFFERSON

Introduction

"What you don't know," the somewhat obscure English writer Sydney Smith (1771–1845) once noted, "would make a great book."

And what you don't know about great books would make a really great book!

So here it is: *what you need to know about* the world's great books and writers but never learned. Using the quick-quiz format that was the hallmark of the *New York Times* bestseller *Don't Know Much About*® *Anything*, this book offers a fun and entertaining way to learn about those books and authors you were supposed to read in high school and college—but probably never did. While serving as a quick refresher course, the book may also introduce you to some writers and works that might not be familiar but should be.

A compendium of fun and fascinating quizzes that will stimulate and inform, *Don't Know Much About Literature* is aimed at reintroducing you to some of the most important writers and their works; explaining what you need to know about hundreds of great books, plays, and poems; exploring less-familiar writers that everyone should know about; and generally rounding out the literary education of readers who have an appetite for learning, but want to have fun doing it.

Emphasizing the household names from literary history, these quizzes focus on major writers and their works, along with some notable books that helped change history—works by Faulkner, Tennessee Williams, and Byron, and Joyce's *Ulysses* among them.

Downbeat about the Beats?

Afraid of Virginia Woolf?

Don't know your Keats from your Yeats?

The book you hold will see you through your most Kafkaesque literary nightmares.

What's more, the book provides fascinating fodder for reading groups and sparkling chatter at cocktail parties. Fills in some gaps in your reader's résumé. Helps out on that literature question in Trivial Pursuit. Inspires a more ambitious summer reading list. *Don't Know Much About Literature* will do all of these things while also providing a challenging quiz that will test even the sharpest know-it-alls.

There's no question about it. Many of us love to read. Like Jefferson, we "cannot live without books." And what's more, we love to talk about reading. This is a book that will have book lovers gloating as they prove just how much they know—or have them sheepishly heading back to the stacks to round out their literary educations.

Do you remember your first books? I do. They were mostly Golden Books, and they filled the foot of my bed. Or do you remember the first book you really loved? Can you remember learning to recite a poem? I had a terribly hard time in sixth grade memorizing Blake's "The Tyger." ("Tyger! Tyger! burning bright / In the forests of the night, / What immortal hand or eye / Could frame thy fearful symmetry?") Did you ever fall in love with a fictional character? Or weep when you finished a book? What book kept you up all night reading?

Of course, if you are what you read, it can be a bit dangerous. When we were compiling this book, an article about books and romance was published in the *New York Times Book Review*. As Rachel Donadio put it, "These days, thanks to social networking sites like Facebook and MySpace, listing your favorite books and authors is a crucial, if risky, part of self-branding. When it comes to online dating, even casual references can turn into deal breakers." One woman, a book critic, told Donadio, "I did have to break up with one guy because he was very keen on Ayn Rand" ("It's Not You, It's Your Books," *New York Times Book Review*, March 30, 2008).

The other story that caught our attention as we compiled our quizzes was a story out of Vermont, where I live and work part of the time. It seems that a few dozen teenagers had been caught partying and vandalizing a small cottage in the Vermont woods. Their doings probably would have gone unnoticed except that the cottage once belonged to Robert Frost. In June 2008, as part of their sentences, the teens were all required to attend a class—taught by the novelist and Middlebury College professor Jay Parini—about the great American poet.

Of course, cynics might laugh and say, "Yes, poetry is punishment." But at the heart of this sentence is a much grander notion. We read to change our lives and our minds. Of course, we read for many reasons— simple pleasure, excitement, a whiff of romance. But at the bottom, I think we read because books can change people. I was a voracious reader as a child, but

I clearly recall the change in my way of looking at the world back in the summer of 1968 when I read Upton Sinclair's *The Jungle* and Dalton Trumbo's *Johnny Got His Gun*. Both books were crucial in opening my eyes to the fact that the world could be very different from the tidy vision I had been working with. Those books accomplished what the brilliant Joseph Conrad once said was the writer's task: "To make you see."

I don't know if this book will bring you to such truths. But I do hope that you will have some fun and get pointed in the right direction. After all, as Jimmy Walker, the colorful Jazz Age mayor of New York City, once put it, "No woman was ever ruined by a book."

Just one note before you start reading and proving how smart you are—or how much you need to learn. You will find very few references to Shakespeare in this collection. It's not that we don't like the Bard. In fact, we do—so much so that we thought the guy deserves his own book. So next up on the schedule of the Don't Know Much About series is a book dedicated to the life, times, poetry, and plays of William Shakespeare.

And yes, we are certain that lots of your other favorite authors or books are missing from this collection. I know I had to leave out some of my favorites (sorry to the late Mr. Updike, who merits only a passing reference). Is there somebody or some book that you think deserves a "quiz of one's own"? Let us know at our Web site DontKnowMuch.com or search "Kenneth C. Davis" on Facebook.

So sharpen your pencils and get ready to test your literary wits.

Don't Know Much About® Literature

DON'T KNOW MUCH ABOUT

Fictional First Lines

Since you can't judge a book by its cover, the first line had better be good. Would Herman Melville have reeled in readers if *Moby-Dick* had not begun with the immortal words, "Call me Ishmael"? See how many of these famous first lines you can identify—just be careful that you don't get hooked.

1. It was love at first sight.

2. It is a truth universally acknowledged, that a single man in possession of a good fortune must be in want of a wife.

3. "Where's Papa going with that ax?"

4. Many years later, as he faced the firing squad, Colonel Aureliano Buendía was to remember

that distant afternoon when his father took him to discover ice.

5. One morning, as Gregor Samsa was waking up from anxious dreams, he discovered that in bed he had been changed into a monstrous, verminous bug.

6. It was the best of times, it was the worst of times . . .

7. Once upon a time and a very good time it was there was a moocow coming down along the road and this moocow that was coming down along the road met a nicens little boy named baby tuckoo . . .

8. You better not never tell nobody but God.

ANSWERS

1. Joseph Heller, *Catch-22*.

2. Jane Austen, *Pride and Prejudice*.

3. E. B. White, *Charlotte's Web*.

4. Gabriel García Márquez, *One Hundred Years of Solitude* (translated by Gregory Rabassa).

5. Franz Kafka, *The Metamorphosis* (translated by Ian Johnson).

6. Charles Dickens, *A Tale of Two Cities*.

7. James Joyce, *A Portrait of the Artist as a Young Man*.

8. Alice Walker, *The Color Purple*.

DON'T KNOW MUCH ABOUT
Charlotte's Web

"*S*alutations!" Spoken from a barn's rafters, this greeting begins one of the most unlikely and special friendships in literature, that between Charlotte A. Cavatica, a spider, and Wilbur, a young pig. In *Charlotte's Web* (1952), Charlotte saves Wilbur from slaughter by spinning words like "TERRIFIC" and "RADIANT" into her web above his pen. The author Elwyn Brooks White (1899–1985), known as Andy to friends and as E. B. White to readers, called *Charlotte's Web* "a story of friendship and salvation on a farm," inspired by the animals in his Maine barn. *Charlotte's Web* was the second of White's three children's books, which punctuated a successful career as a journalist and essayist. Wallow in this quick quiz about the author of one of the best-loved children's books.

1. What is the name of the eight-year-old girl who adopts the newborn Wilbur, saving him from Papa's ax?

2. What is the first message that Charlotte spins into her web?

3. What word does Charlotte write above Wilbur's pen because he is "not proud" and "close to the ground"?

4. *Charlotte's Web* was turned into an animated film in 1973 and into a live-action film with computer animation in 2006. Which other children's classic by E. B. White became a movie with both live action and computer animation?

5. For what nonfiction book is E. B. White best known?

6. What is White's third and final children's book?

ANSWERS

1. Fern Arable.

2. SOME PIG.

3. HUMBLE.

4. *Stuart Little*, published in 1945.

5. *The Elements of Style.* White's sharp observations of modern life were staples of the *New Yorker*'s "Talk of the Town" column for decades, and he distilled his guidelines for writing clearly and elegantly in the book, originally written by his Cornell professor, William Strunk Jr.

6. *The Trumpet of the Swan* (1970).

DON'T KNOW MUCH ABOUT
Dracula

F ew books have captured readers' imaginations as *Dracula* did, spawning hundreds of books and movies, not to mention uncountable cape-and-fangs Halloween costumes. Published in 1897 in Victorian England, the novel blended the folklore of vampires and other bloodsucking creatures with Catholic traditions, scraps of Romanian history, and many of Bram Stoker's own inventions. Born Abraham Stoker in Dublin, Ireland, Stoker (1847–1912) wrote *Dracula* as a novel told through journals, letters, and fictional news clippings to lend his fantastical horror story a realistic feel—and the novel's contemporary setting added to its chilling authenticity. Sink your teeth into this *Dracula* quiz.

TRUE OR FALSE?

1. Bram Stoker took Count Dracula's name from the fifteenth-century Romanian prince Vladislav III, better known as "Vlad the Impaler."

2. In Stoker's novel, before Count Dracula transforms Lucy into a vampire, he famously whispers, "I want to suck your blood."

3. Stoker drew the following details from eastern European vampire folklore: vampires can't come into a house uninvited; they can take the shape of wolves; garlic and crosses repulse vampires; they can be killed by a stake through the heart.

4. Some scholars cite the influences of Celtic vampire legends on *Dracula*.

5. Bram Stoker's *Dracula* popularized the notion that sunlight was harmful to vampires.

ANSWERS

1. True. Vlad the Impaler, born in Transylvania in 1431, was called "Dracula," or "Son of Dracul." His father, Vladislav II, was nicknamed "Dracul," meaning "devil" and "dragon"—not for evil deeds, but because he belonged to the Order of the Dragon, a secret fraternity of knights whose mission was to protect the Holy Roman Empire from Ottoman invasion. In early drafts, Stoker's character was named "Count Wampyr."

2. False. Dracula never says this line in Bram Stoker's novel. In fact, even the Hungarian actor Béla Lugosi didn't say "I vant to suck your blood" in the classic 1931 movie version, though this line is often quoted as his.

3. True. These details were the result of Stoker's extensive research.

4. True. Although Stoker's interest in Slavic vampires is well documented, scholars have suggested that Stoker, an Irish writer, was also inspired by Celtic folklore involving vampiric chieftains and bloodsucking fairies.

5. False. This was an invention of F. W. Murnau's 1922 movie *Nosferatu*, an unauthorized film version of *Dracula*.

DON'T KNOW MUCH ABOUT
Ernest Hemingway

They called him "Papa." One of America's most successful and admired novelists, Ernest Hemingway (1899–1961) once compared his bare-bones style to an iceberg: "There is seven-eighths of it under water for every part that shows." Beneath Hemingway's famously understated prose, which often celebrated such traditionally masculine pursuits as combat, hunting, and boxing, his heroes encountered doubt, isolation, and failure. Wounded as an ambulance driver during World War I and shaken by his experience of the war, Hemingway moved to Paris in 1921 and joined a circle of similarly disenchanted young writers, including F. Scott Fitzgerald and John Dos Passos. Hemingway's breakthrough novel, *The Sun Also Rises*, popularized a phrase borrowed from the author Gertrude Stein: the

"Lost Generation." See if you can find answers to these questions about the great Lost Generation author who took his own life with a shotgun blast.

1. Before Hemingway turned to fiction, what job helped develop his spare writing style?

2. What recurring, semiautobiographical Hemingway hero was first featured in the 1924 story collection *In Our Time*?

3. In *A Farewell to Arms,* how does the main character Frederic Henry serve during World War I?

4. What is the subject of Hemingway's 1932 nonfiction book, *Death in the Afternoon*? (Hint: It's also prominently featured in his 1926 novel, *The Sun Also Rises*.)

5. Which Hemingway work contains the famous line, "Man is not made for defeat. A man can be destroyed but not defeated"?

6. What was Hemingway's oft-cited definition of "guts"?

ANSWERS

1. Newspaperman. Fresh out of high school, the seventeen-year-old Hemingway took a job as a junior reporter for the *Kansas City Star*. He later worked as a foreign correspondent covering wars in Europe.

2. Nick Adams. Often read as an alter ego for Hemingway, Nick Adams is a prototype for many later Hemingway characters, as well as the protagonist of the posthumously published collection *The Nick Adams Stories* (1972).

3. Just as Hemingway himself served: as an ambulance driver on the Italian front.

4. Spanish bullfighting.

5. *The Old Man and the Sea* (1952).

6. "Grace under pressure."

DON'T KNOW MUCH ABOUT
Emily Dickinson

One of America's most enigmatic poets, Emily Dickinson (1830–1886) spent the last twenty years of her life as a recluse, rarely leaving the home in Amherst, Massachusetts, where she was born. She greeted guests from behind a door, used a basket and cord to lower cookies out her window to local children, and, after her father's death in 1874, dressed entirely in white. As a young woman, Dickinson studied botany and the classics, then spent a lonely year at Mount Holyoke Female Seminary, where she was ostracized for refusing to declare her faith in Christ. Rather than teach or marry—the acceptable options in her day for women of her class—Dickinson stayed home and wrote nearly two thousand poems, largely unpublished in her lifetime. After her death in 1886, her sister Lavinia found forty fascicles, hand-sewn booklets containing more than eight hundred unseen poems. After faithfully burning thousands of Emily's letters, Lavinia helped publish the poems—the first of which saw print in 1890. Immediately recognizable for their short lines broken by dashes, Dickinson's poems speak of solitude and death, as well as of imagination, passion, immortality, and childlike wonder with the world. What do you know about the "Woman in White"? Take this quiz and see.

1. What popular song contains the line, "And you read your Emily Dickinson / And I my Robert Frost"?

2. How many of Dickinson's poems were published in her lifetime?

3. Although Dickinson's uses of meter and rhyme were innovative, what type of song inspired the rhythm and form of her poems?

4. What cult movie briefly features a giant puppet of Emily Dickinson?

ANSWERS

1. "Dangling Conversation," written by Paul Simon.

2. Seven. Some scholars argue only six, claiming that one poem was published in two versions.

3. Hymns.

4. *Being John Malkovich.* The main character's rival puppeteer stages William Luce's one-woman play *The Belle of Amherst* off a bridge with a four-story-tall marionette.

DON'T KNOW MUCH ABOUT
John Steinbeck

B orn in Salinas, California, in 1902, John Steinbeck built his reputation writing about the struggles of down-and-out people: Dust Bowl farmers and pearl divers, prostitutes, jobless migrants, and Depression-era hoboes. In later years Steinbeck signed all his letters with a "pigasus" logo: a funny stamp of a little round pig with wings. Around the pig, Steinbeck added the words *Ad astra per alia porci*, or "To the stars on the wings of a pig"—an apt motto for an author who portrayed the goodness, even holiness, of the common man. Take this quick quiz about John Steinbeck, who died in 1968—just don't cry sour grapes if you're stumped.

1. **What did Steinbeck study at Stanford? (Hint: He returned to this subject in his 1941 nonfic-**

tion book *Sea of Cortez*, written with Edward F. Ricketts.)

2. Who wrote and performed the song "The Ballad of Tom Joad," inspired by the main character in *The Grapes of Wrath*?

3. What biblical story inspired the family drama in *East of Eden*?

4. Which of John Steinbeck's novels have been adapted into Oscar-winning films?

5. Steinbeck wrote the screenplay for what biopic (for which Anthony Quinn won an Oscar for best supporting actor)?

ANSWERS

1. Marine biology.

2. Woody Guthrie. Bruce Springsteen also wrote a song inspired by *The Grapes of Wrath*: "The Ghost of Tom Joad," released on an album of the same name.

3. The story of Cain and Abel.

4. *The Grapes of Wrath* (1940) won two Oscars—for best supporting actress and for best director—out of seven nominations. *East of Eden* (1955) won an Oscar for best supporting actress. *Of Mice and Men* (1939), *Tortilla Flat* (1942), *Lifeboat* (1944—based on a Steinbeck short story), and *A Medal for Benny* (1945—another short story) all received Academy Award nominations.

5. *Viva Zapata!*

DON'T KNOW MUCH ABOUT
Books in Hollywood

Which did you like better—the book or the movie? Books-turned-film, from *Gone with the Wind* to *Harry Potter*, have delighted and (perhaps more often) frustrated bookworms: "Rhett Butler played by Clark Gable, a *Northerner?*" or "The story of Voldemort had *way* more detail in the book!" But there are plenty of films that you may not even realize are based on books, such as the masterworks of Akira Kurosawa, who turned Shakespeare's *Macbeth* and *King Lear* into the samurai classics *Throne of Blood* and *Ran*. See if you can name the great books behind the silver screen . . . then get back to arguing over the book versus the movie.

1. Clueless (directed by Amy Heckerling, 1995)

2. *O Brother, Where Art Thou?* (directed by Joel Coen, 2000)

3. *Apocalypse Now* (directed by Francis Ford Coppola, 1979)

4. *She's All That* (directed by Robert Iscove, 1999)

5. *Blade Runner* (directed by Ridley Scott, 1982)

ANSWERS

1. *Emma,* by Jane Austen.

2. The *Odyssey,* by Homer.

3. *Heart of Darkness,* by Joseph Conrad.

4. *Pygmalion,* by George Bernard Shaw.

5. *Do Androids Dream of Electric Sheep?,* by Philip K. Dick.

DON'T KNOW MUCH ABOUT
Gone with the Wind

Pansy O'Hara. Just doesn't sound right, does it? That's what Margaret Mitchell (1900–1949) had named her heroine in the initial version of *Gone with the Wind* (1936), the hit book that almost wasn't. A newspaper reporter, Mitchell tried her hand at writing fiction while she recovered from a horseback-riding accident. Ashamed of the novel, she kept it secret from her closest friends—until one of them egged her on by suggesting that she probably couldn't write a successful novel. Mitchell impulsively delivered the manuscript to an eager editor, and the rest is history: Pansy became Scarlett, *Gone with the Wind* won readers' hearts (and the 1937 Pulitzer), and on the silver screen Clark Gable told Vivien Leigh, "Frankly, my dear, I don't give a damn." If you do—give a damn, that is—take this quick *Gone with the Wind* quiz.

1. After *Gone with the Wind*, what was Mitchell's bestselling novel?

2. What word was changed or added to Rhett Butler's most famous line in the film version ("Frankly, my dear, I don't give a damn")?

3. What was Alexandra Ripley's 1991 *Gone with the Wind* sequel called?

4. What 2001 parallel novel recast *Gone with the Wind* from the point of view of Cynara, Scarlett's mixed-race half sister?

5. Why was Hattie McDaniel, the first African American to win an Oscar—she won the Oscar for best supporting actress for her role in the movie version of *Gone with the Wind*—unable to attend the movie's premiere?

ANSWERS

1. There wasn't one—Mitchell published only one novel in her lifetime.

2. "Frankly." In the book, Rhett tells Scarlett, "My dear, I don't give a damn."

3. *Scarlett.*

4. *The Wind Done Gone,* by Alice Randall.

5. The movie theater was segregated.

DON'T KNOW MUCH ABOUT
George Orwell

Big Brother is watching you.

These famous words conjure up the nightmare of George Orwell's *1984*—a bleak future where everyone is under government surveillance. Born Eric Arthur Blair in 1903, Orwell is best known for his novels warning readers about the dangers of totalitarianism. Set in a barnyard, *Animal Farm* (1945) was a satire of Soviet Communism: the animals revolt and overthrow the farmers, only to create another unfair society, the only difference being that this time the pigs are the masters. *1984*—published in 1949, a year before Orwell's death—was a cautionary tale about a world of endless war. A government called "the Party" brainwashes its citizens to believe that "War is Peace. Freedom is Slavery. Ignorance is Strength." If you don't agree with the Party about ignorance, take this quick quiz and learn a little more about Orwell.

TRUE OR FALSE?

1. George Orwell was born in India.

2. After high school, Orwell worked as a labor organizer in northern England.

3. Eric Arthur Blair took the pen name "George Orwell" to conceal his class background, especially his upper-crust education.

4. Orwell was almost killed during World War II.

5. Orwell created and broadcast war propaganda for Britain.

ANSWERS

1. True. Orwell was born to British parents in Mothari, Bengal, where his father worked in the government's Opium Department. His mother moved him to England a year later.

2. False. After graduating from the prestigious boarding school Eton, Orwell joined the British police force in Burma, where he served for five years. The experience sharpened his mistrust of people in power and inspired his first novel, *Burmese Days*.

3. True. Blair became "George Orwell" in 1933 with the publication of *Down and Out in London and Paris*, not wanting his Eton education to skew readers' opinions of this book about poverty.

4. False. But Orwell was indeed injured fighting in the Spanish Civil War. In December 1936, Orwell joined an anarchist unit of the Republicans in Spain, fighting the fascist Nationalists led by Francisco Franco. The following May, he was shot through the neck—an injury that almost cost him his life.

5. True. From 1941 to 1943 he was a radio broad-caster to India for the BBC. Orwell's experience creating propaganda inspired ideas like "double-speak" and the "Ministry of Truth" in *1984.*

DON'T KNOW MUCH ABOUT
Greek Tragedies

Dionysus, the Greek god of wine and intoxication, may have been the party animal of the Olympians, but he's also associated closely with tragedy. The first dramas, especially tragedies, were performed at yearly celebrations of Dionysus in ancient Greece. (In fact, the word "tragedy" comes from the Greek word for "goat," an animal sacred to Dionysus.) Aeschylus (525–456 BCE), Sophocles (c. 496–406 BCE), and Euripides (c. 484–406 BCE) have endured as masters of this art, which the philosopher Aristotle (384–322 BCE) defined as "a form of drama exciting the emotions of pity and fear" in order to cause a cleansing, or "catharsis," of these feelings. Now grab some Kleenex and test your knowledge of the classic tragedies with this quick quiz.

1. Which tragic hero, featured in plays by Sophocles, fulfills an oracle's prediction that he will kill his father and marry his mother?

2. Which 1942 play, inspired by a Sophocles tragedy of the same name, was an allegory of France under the pro-Nazi Vichy government?

3. In Aeschylus's play *Prometheus Bound*, why is the titan Prometheus fastened to a mountain?

4. Which character from Greek mythology—a woman who helped her brother kill their mother, Clytemnestra—appears in plays by Euripides, Sophocles, and Aeschylus?

5. Which complicated character—a sorceress who murders her children—is the heroine of a Euripides play?

ANSWERS

1. Oedipus. A character from Greek myth, he is the subject of Sophocles' plays *Oedipus Rex* and *Oedipus at Colonus*. The psychoanalyst Sigmund Freud used the term "Oedipus complex" to describe the childhood conflict of a boy's attraction to his mother and feelings of rivalry with his father.

2. *Antigone*, by Jean Anouilh. The play, about a girl who faces a death sentence for defying the king, was first produced in Nazi-occupied Paris in 1944.

3. Zeus is punishing Prometheus for stealing fire from the heavens and giving it to humans.

4. Electra. She is the title character of Sophocles' *Electra* and Euripides' *Electra*, and she is a major character in Aeschylus's *Libation Bearers* in his *Oresteia* trilogy.

5. Medea, in the play of the same title.

DON'T KNOW MUCH ABOUT
Poetic First Lines

"**L**et us go then, you and I." With this opening line, T. S. Eliot invites his reader into the mind of his uninspired, indecisive narrator in "The Love Song of J. Alfred Prufrock." A poem's first line can set a scene, as Walt Whitman's "When lilacs last in the dooryard bloomed" does. Or it might intrigue the reader, as when Emily Dickinson writes, "I heard a Fly buzz— when I died" (Poem 465). Who opened their poems with the famous lines below? See how many poets you can identify.

1. **How do I love thee? Let me count the ways.**

2. **anyone lived in a pretty how town**

3. **Take up the White Man's burden—**

4. 'Twas brillig, and the slithy toves

5. In Xanadu did Kubla Kahn

6. It so happens I am sick of being a man.

7. I saw the best minds of my generation destroyed by madness, starving hysterical naked,

ANSWERS

1. Elizabeth Barrett Browning, "Sonnet 43."

2. e. e. cummings, "anyone lived in a pretty how town."

3. Rudyard Kipling, "The White Man's Burden." This 1899 poem encouraged Americans to colonize the Philippines and other former Spanish colonies.

4. Lewis Carroll, "Jabberwocky," from *Through the Looking-Glass, and What Alice Found There.*

5. Samuel Taylor Coleridge, "Kubla Kahn."

6. Pablo Neruda, "Walking Around" (translated by Robert Bly).

7. Allen Ginsberg, "Howl."

DON'T KNOW MUCH ABOUT
Robert Frost

Apples, birches, hayfields, and stone walls: simple features like these make up the landscape of four-time Pultizer Prize winner Robert Frost's poetry. Known as a poet of New England, Frost (1874–1963) spent much of his life working and wandering the woods and farmland of Massachusetts, Vermont, and New Hampshire. Frost's language is plain and straight-forward, his lines inspired by the laconic speech of his Yankee neighbors. But although poems like "Stopping by Woods on a Snowy Evening" are accessible enough to make Frost a grammar-school favorite, his poetry is contemplative and sometimes dark—concerned with themes like growing old and facing death. Stop here a moment and take this Frost quiz.

1. In what city was Robert Frost born?

2. What Yankee saying does Frost's neighbor repeat in the poem "Mending Wall"?

3. Which president chose Frost to read a poem at his inauguration?

4. At that inauguration, why did Frost recite "The Gift Outright"?

5. What bestselling self-help book took its title from a Robert Frost poem?

6. In a poem, Frost wrote his own epitaph. What is it?

ANSWERS

1. San Francisco, California.

2. "Good fences make good neighbors."

3. John F. Kennedy, in January 1961.

4. Frost had written a new poem called "Dedication," but he couldn't read it in the January glare. So instead he recited the 1942 poem "The Gift Outright," which he knew by heart.

5. *The Road Less Traveled,* by M. Scott Peck.

6. "I had a lover's quarrel with the world."

DON'T KNOW MUCH ABOUT
Pen Names

What's in a name? A rose by any other name might smell as sweet, but many authors choose to take on a nom de plume for a variety of reasons. Historically, some women wrote under men's names so that their work would be taken more seriously—especially in the nineteenth century, when Nathaniel Hawthorne complained about that "damned mob of scribbling women" whose novels were so popular. Mary Ann Evans, the author of *Middlemarch* who is better known as George Eliot, was one such novelist. Other authors published under pseudonyms to keep their professions or writing genres separate; this was the case for the mathematician Charles Dodgson, who wrote *Alice's Adventures in Wonderland* as Lewis Carroll. Edward Gorey, known for his darkly comic illustrated books, took dozens of pseudonyms, most of them scrambled versions of his name—like Ogdred Weary, Dogear Wryde, and E. G. Deadworry. See how many better-known-as authors you can identify by their given names.

1. **Neftalí Ricardo Reyes Basoalto**

2. **Samuel Clemens**

3. **Karen Blixen**

4. **François-Marie Arouet**

5. **William Sydney Porter**

6. **Józef Teodor Konrad Korzeniowski**

ANSWERS

1. Pablo Neruda. He took on the surname "Neruda" in homage to the Czech poet Jan Neruda.

2. Mark Twain. Clemens may have taken his pen name from a riverboater's expression: "mark twain!" meant that the water was deep enough for safe passage.

3. Isak Dinesen, author of *Out of Africa*.

4. Voltaire, author of *Candide*.

5. O. Henry.

6. Joseph Conrad.

DON'T KNOW MUCH ABOUT
Franz Kafka

Born in 1883 to a middle-class Jewish family in Prague, Franz Kafka lived a life of suffering: depression and anxiety, migraines, insomnia, constipation and boils, boring jobs at an insurance agency and then an asbestos company, several broken marriage engagements, and a struggle with tuberculosis that ended in 1924 with his death. His fiction showed his melancholy. Ordinary happiness escapes his characters, who find themselves trapped in mazelike situations so inexplicable, frustrating, and absurd that they can only be described as "Kafkaesque." Though some find dark humor and even playfulness in Kafka's writing, others see only existential anguish and the fruitless search for meaning in life. Test your own knowledge of all things Kafkaesque with this quiz.

1. At the beginning of Kafka's novella *The Metamorphosis* (1915), what change does Gregor Samsa notice upon waking up?

2. Into what format did Peter Kuper adapt *The Metamorphosis* in 2003?

3. In *The Trial,* what crime did Joseph K. commit?

4. Many of Kafka's main characters have telling names that suggest connections to Kafka himself. What is the name of the land surveyor in *The Castle,* who is repeatedly denied entrance to the castle he must survey?

5. What was Kafka's request to his friend Max Brod regarding his unpublished writing?

ANSWERS

1. That he has been transformed into a gigantic, beetle-like insect.

2. Graphic novel.

3. None. He is arrested for no reason as soon as he wakes up.

4. K.

5. That Brod burn it. Instead, Brod edited and published everything, both Kafka's journals and his works, including *The Castle* and *The Trial*. During Kafka's life, he had reluctantly published only a few stories, such as *The Metamorphosis*.

DON'T KNOW MUCH ABOUT
Agatha Christie

The "Queen of Crime," Dame Agatha Christie (1890–1976) is one of the bestselling and most widely translated writers of all time. In her lifetime, she published more than eighty novels and short-story collections, along with a dozen plays. Christie's intricate mysteries were matched only by her clever protagonists, such as the Belgian detective Hercule Poirot, who relied upon the power of his "little grey cells." Another of Christie's well-loved sleuths was the amateur detective Jane Marple, an elderly spinster who could crack the cases that stumped Scotland Yard. Christie claimed that Miss Marple was inspired by her real-life grandmother, who "expected the worst of everyone and everything and was with almost frightening accuracy, usually proved right." Test your own little grey cells with this Christie quiz . . . then you can get back to figuring out whodunit.

1. **What was the first Christie novel to feature Miss Marple?**

2. **Who is the only fictional character ever to receive a front-page obituary in the *New York Times*?**

3. **What is the longest continuously running theater production in history?**

4. **What 1932 news event inspired the plot of *Murder on the Orient Express*?**

5. **With what title was *And Then There Were None*, Christie's bestselling book, first published?**

ANSWERS

1. *Murder at the Vicarage* (1930).

2. Hercule Poirot.

3. *The Mousetrap.* It has been running in London since 1952.

4. The kidnapping of the Lindbergh baby. The infant son of the aviator Charles A. Lindbergh and Anne Morrow Lindbergh was kidnapped and murdered despite the $50,000 ransom that the Lindberghs had paid.

5. *Ten Little Niggers* (1939). This title was changed for the first U.S. edition, published in 1940. Alternate versions of the book printed the children's rhyme in chapter 2 as "Ten Little Indians," and in an attempt to be less controversial, "Ten Little Soldier Boys."

DON'T KNOW MUCH ABOUT
Moby-Dick

"Thar she blows!" *Moby-Dick*, Herman Melville's sprawling masterpiece, is the epic story of a whaling ship, the *Pequod*, in search of a white whale notorious for sinking whalers. The ship's captain, Ahab, pursues his singular obsession to destroy Moby-Dick, who took his leg on a previous voyage, while the book's narrator, Ishmael, provides keen observations of his monomaniacal captain, his crewmates, whaling, and cetology (the study of whales). Melville could write of life on a whaling boat with such rich detail because he had spent eighteen months aboard the *Acushnet* on a whaling voyage to the South Seas—where he jumped ship, spent time with alleged cannibals, participated in a failed mutiny, and escaped a Tahitian jail. In fact, Melville (1819–1891) was much better known during his lifetime for *Typee* and *Omoo,* two crowd-pleasing South Seas adventures based on his real-life experiences. Take this *Moby-Dick* quiz to see whether you're an old salt like Ahab or a green hand like Ishmael.

1. What is the name of Ishmael's bedfellow and the *Pequod*'s chief harpooner, a native of the fictitious Polynesian island Kokovoko?

2. What type of whale is Moby-Dick?

3. True or false: Moby-Dick was based on an actual white whale nicknamed "Mocha Dick."

4. What town—the whaling port from which the *Pequod* departs in Melville's novel—holds a *Moby-Dick* reading marathon every year?

5. What American science-fiction writer cowrote the screenplay for John Huston's 1956 film version of *Moby-Dick?*

ANSWERS

1. Queequeg.

2. A sperm whale—the only whale type known to have deliberately sunk ships.

3. True. Mocha Dick was a massive white sperm whale who roamed off the coast of Chile in the mid-nineteenth century and who had a reputation for destroying boats.

4. New Bedford, Massachusetts. The marathon lasts about twenty-five hours!

5. Ray Bradbury of *Martian Chronicles* and *Fahrenheit 451* fame.

DON'T KNOW MUCH ABOUT
The Canterbury Tales

Corruption, adultery, drunkenness, and deceit: *The Canterbury Tales* has it all. And for high school students who get past the Middle English, the nighttime hijinks, butt jokes, and slapstick comedy of stories like "The Miller's Tale" might just seem fit for the *American Pie* movies. Geoffrey Chaucer (d. 1400), who was born in London in the 1340s and came of age at the height of the Black Death, frames the collection as tales told by pilgrims on their way to Canterbury Cathedral. These pilgrims are a cross section of medieval life, from the chivalric Knight to the bawdy Miller to the five-times-married Wife of Bath, who some scholars have called one of English literature's first feminists. See how much you know about what happened "Whan that Aprill with his shoures soote / The droghte of

March hath perced to the roote" with this *Canterbury Tales* quiz.

1. What, does the narrator joke, is the Doctor's favorite medicine?

2. Which pilgrim claims that he cannot be held accountable for his inappropriate tale, because he is so drunk?

3. How does the Pardoner make a living?

4. According to the tale told by the Wife of Bath, what is the one thing all women want?

5. Which 2001 film, starring Heath Ledger, featured Paul Bettany as Geoffrey Chaucer?

ANSWERS

1. Gold. (Some things never change!)

2. The Miller.

3. He sells indulgences—in other words, people pay him to forgive their sins. He also sells religious "relics" that he admits to the other pilgrims are fake.

4. To be in charge of their husbands.

5. *A Knight's Tale.*

DON'T KNOW MUCH ABOUT
Books on Broadway

How do you solve a problem like Maria? How do you catch a cloud and pin it down? And how do you turn a book into a hit Broadway musical? *The Sound of Music*, which debuted on Broadway in 1959 (the movie version came out in 1965), began with Maria von Trapp's memoir *The Story of the Trapp Family Singers* (1949). The memoir inspired two successful German films in the 1950s, which in turn inspired the Broadway producers Leland Hayward and Richard Halliday to commission a stage adaptation by the playwrights Howard Lindsay and Russel Crouse. Hayward and Halliday decided that rather than use the Trapp family's own music, they would add numbers by Richard Rodgers and Oscar Hammerstein II, the team behind *Oklahoma!*, *South Pacific*, and *The King and I*.

The Sound of Music, of course, became a smashing success. Many other musical adaptations have proved that "once you know the notes to sing, you can sing most anything." See if you can identify the novels, nonmusical plays, and even one book of poems behind these catchy Broadway shows.

1. *The Man of La Mancha*

2. *My Fair Lady*

3. *West Side Story*

4. *The Phantom of the Opera*

5. *Cats!*

6. *South Pacific*

ANSWERS

1. *Don Quixote*, the novel by Miguel de Cervantes.

2. *Pygmalion*, the play by George Bernard Shaw. The play itself is based on the tale of Pygmalion— about a sculptor who falls in love with a woman he has carved from ivory—in Ovid's *Metamorphoses*.

3. *Romeo and Juliet*, the play by William Shakespeare.

4. *Le fantôme de l'opéra*, the novel by Gaston Leroux.

5. *Old Possum's Book of Practical Cats*, a book of poems by T. S. Eliot.

6. *Tales of the South Pacific*, James Michener's Pulitzer Prize–winning story collection.

DON'T KNOW MUCH ABOUT
Tennessee Williams

*Whoever you are—I have always depended on
the kindness of strangers.*

The departing words of Blanche DuBois in *A Street-car Named Desire* (1947) are now legendary. But before Vivien Leigh and Marlon Brando's iconic portrayals of the fallen Southern belle and her brother-in-law Stanley Kowalski, those characters sprang from the pen of the American playwright Tennessee Williams (1911–1983). Like many of Williams's plays, *A Streetcar Named Desire* buzzed with the sexual tension and latent violence beneath the surface of everyday life. Desire to test your knowledge of Williams and his plays? Hop a ride to this quick quiz, and you might learn something along the way.

1. **Was Williams actually from Tennessee?**

2. In *A Streetcar Named Desire*, what is the name of Blanche DuBois's sister?

3. Tennessee Williams called his breakout success a "memory play," and suggested that its experimental approach might present "a more penetrating and vivid expression of things as they are." Which play was he describing?

4. Williams won his first Pulitzer for *A Streetcar Named Desire*. Which play won him his second?

5. Which 1953 Williams play featured as characters Don Quixote and Sancho Panza, the legendary lover Casanova, and Kilroy, the American GI of graffiti fame?

6. Which of his plays did Williams rewrite as *Orpheus Descending* (1957)?

ANSWERS

1. No, but his father was, and that's where he got the nickname. The playwright was born Thomas Lanier Williams in Columbus, Mississippi.

2. Stella Kowalski. "Stella! Hey, Stella!" was ranked #45 on the American Film Institute's "100 Years . . . 100 Movie Quotes" list. "I have always depended on the kindness of strangers" came in at #75.

3. *The Glass Menagerie* (1944), which won the New York Drama Critics' Circle Award for the best play of 1945.

4. *Cat on a Hot Tin Roof* (1955).

5. *Camino Real.*

6. *Battle of Angels,* which was poorly received in 1940.

DON'T KNOW MUCH ABOUT
Gabriel García Márquez

Amaster of magic realism, the Colombian author
Gabriel García Márquez (b. 1928) weaves history and fantasy together to create surreal fictions and
enchanted Latin American landscapes. *Cien años de
soledad* (1967; English trans., *One Hundred Years of
Solitude*, 1970) follows the century-long epic of the
Buendía family, from their founding of the town of
Macondo in the jungle to their apocalyptic end, fore-
told in a gypsy's history book. Alongside plagues of insomnia and amnesia, a four-year-long rainstorm, and a
realization that time flows in circles, García Márquez
parallels real-life events in this fiction: contact with
other villages leads to civil war, a railroad carries grin-
gos who start a company town, and the army massacres
striking banana workers. García Márquez explained

that this mix of mythical and historical storytelling "was based on the way my grandmother used to tell stories," saying fantastic things as if they were perfectly normal.

1. Which Latin American political figure is the subject of García Márquez's novel *The General in His Labyrinth*?

2. In his acceptance speech for the 1982 Nobel Prize in Literature, which former Nobel laureate did García Márquez call "my master"?

3. In *The Autumn of the Patriarch*, what resource does García Márquez's fictional dictator sell to the United States?

4. In a failed 2006 referendum, what did the mayor of Aracataca, Colombia, suggest renaming the town, which is García Márquez's birthplace?

5. What influential European author did García Márquez compare to his grandmother, for saying "the wildest things with a completely natural tone of voice"?

ANSWERS

1. Simón Bolívar.

2. William Faulkner.

3. The sea.

4. Aracataca-Macondo.

5. Franz Kafka.

DON'T KNOW MUCH ABOUT
Nobel Firsts

Ever heard of Sully Prudhomme? His popularity hasn't stood the test of time, but in 1901 this Frenchman was awarded the first-ever Nobel Prize in Literature for "lofty idealism, artistic perfection, and a rare combination of the qualities of both heart and intellect" in his poetry. The twentieth century saw a lot of literary laureate firsts—so don't waste a second in answering these Nobel quiz questions.

1. **Who was the first woman to win a Nobel Prize in Literature?**

2. **Who was the first American writer to win?**

3. **Who was the first English-language writer to win?**

4. Who was the first Irishman to win?

5. Who was the first Latin American writer to win?

6. Who was the first African American writer to win?

7. Who was the first American woman to win?

ANSWERS

1. Selma Lagerlöf, 1909.

2. Sinclair Lewis, 1930.

3. Rudyard Kipling, 1907.

4. William Butler Yeats, 1923.

5. Chile's Gabriela Mistral, 1945.

6. Toni Morrison, 1993.

7. Pearl S. Buck, 1938.

DON'T KNOW MUCH ABOUT
Charles Dickens

Uriah Heep, the unctuous clerk at David Copperfield's 'umble service. Miss Havisham, the
old spinster in a wedding dress, locked in her man-
sion full of stopped clocks. Fresh-faced Nicholas
Nickleby, making his way in the world. Eccentric
Betsy Trotwood and sweetly naive Dora Spenlow.
Coldhearted Ebenezer Scrooge and poor little Tiny
Tim. Charles Dickens (1812–1870) peopled his fifteen
novels—ten of which weigh in at more than eight hundred pages!—with one of the most colorful and memorable casts of characters in all of literature. Test your
knowledge of Charles Dickens by figuring out which
of the statements below are true—if they're false, just
say "Bah, humbug!"

TRUE OR FALSE?

1. Novels like *Oliver Twist*, with their harsh realism, spawned the colloquialism "as the dickens"—as in, for instance, "It's cold as the dickens in here!"

2. In Dickens's time, England's New Poor Law actually contained feeding regulations—the ones that Oliver Twist violates when he asks Mr. Bumble for "more."

3. In the Victorian spirit of charity, Dickens helped found and run a home for former prostitutes called "Urania Cottage."

4. Charles Dickens ends many of his chapters with cliff-hangers and nail-biters—this is because most of his work was published in serial form, one episode or installment at a time.

ANSWERS

1. False. "Dickens" is simply a euphemism for "devil," and the word first appears in print in the work of another English literary titan: William Shakespeare's *The Merry Wives of Winsor.*

2. True.

3. True.

4. True.

DON'T KNOW MUCH ABOUT
Dystopias

In 1516 a thinker named Sir Thomas More dreamed up an island called "Utopia"—its name in Greek means "not a place"—where greed, irrational thinking, and religious intolerance did not exist. Back on the island of Britain, however, More was beheaded by King Henry VIII in 1535. Perhaps inspired by More's fate, many later authors have instead created pessimistic "dystopias"—the name comes from the Greek roots *dys*, meaning "bad," and *topos*, or place. The bread and butter of science-fiction writing, dystopias often envision corrupt governments, invasive technologies, and dehumanized citizens. The best dystopias show readers elements of their own lives, projected alarmingly into a bleak future. See how many of these "brave new worlds" you can identify based on the descriptions below.

1. Which dystopia, begun by its author in 1948, takes place in the former Great Britain—which is now part of "Airstrip One"?

2. In which novel do citizens worship Ford and pop tablets of *soma* to get happy?

3. Which young-adult novel depicts a society based on the philosophy of "Sameness," where people feel no pain and see only in black and white?

4. In which dystopian novel do firemen like Guy Montag start fires instead of putting them out?

5. Which novel imagines that under capitalism, humans evolve into two separate races—one of which dwells below ground?

6. Bonus question: Sir Thomas More is the central character in what notable piece of literature?

ANSWERS

1. *1984*, by George Orwell (1949).

2. *Brave New World*, by Aldous Huxley (1932).

3. *The Giver*, by Lois Lowry (1993).

4. *Fahrenheit 451*, by Ray Bradbury (1953).

5. *The Time Machine*, by H. G. Wells (1895).

6. He is the subject of Robert Bolt's play, later made into a film, *A Man for All Seasons*.

DON'T KNOW MUCH ABOUT
Edith Wharton

Romance, scandal, and ruin among New York socialites—long before this was the stuff of *People* and *Us Weekly*, it was the subject matter for Edith Wharton's most famous stories. In novels like *The Age of Innocence* (1920) and *The House of Mirth* (1905), as Wharton (1862–1937) painted detailed portraits of high society life, she created heartbreaking conflicts beneath the facade of wealth and manners. Again and again, characters like Newland Archer and Lily Bart are forced to choose between conforming to social expectations and pursuing true love and happiness. Think you can take *A Backwards Glance* at Edith Wharton? Take this quick quiz and test your knowledge.

TRUE OR FALSE?

1. Edith Wharton wrote about wealthy New Yorkers to escape the poverty of her own upbringing.

2. Wharton's *Here and Beyond* (1926), along with several other books, was a collection of ghost stories.

3. Though Edith Wharton was unhappily married, she could not get divorced because doing so was socially unacceptable.

4. In addition to her fiction, Wharton published several books on interior decorating and landscaping.

ANSWERS

1. False. Wharton was born to wealthy New Yorkers and summered in Newport, Rhode Island. She grew up traveling through Europe and was educated by private tutors. After an official debut into society, she married a rich banker twelve years her senior.

2. True.

3. False. She divorced Teddy Wharton in 1913.

4. True.

DON'T KNOW MUCH ABOUT
Fictional Places

W hich way is Wonderland? Through Lewis Carroll's looking glass, of course. How do you get to Narnia? Pick up a C. S. Lewis book and step into the old wardrobe. And everyone knows that to get to the Emerald City, you just follow L. Frank Baum's yellow brick road. So which authors would you have to read to visit the fictional places below?

1. **Mordor and Gondor**

2. **St. Mary Mead**

3. **Yoknapatawpha County**

4. **Earthsea**

5. **Brobdingnab**

6. *Treasure Island*

7. *Macondo*

8. *Alifbay*

9. *Llareggub*

ANSWERS

1. J. R. R. Tolkien.

2. Agatha Christie.

3. William Faulkner.

4. Ursula K. Le Guin.

5. Jonathan Swift.

6. Robert Louis Stevenson.

7. Gabriel García Márquez.

8. Salman Rushdie.

9. Dylan Thomas.

DON'T KNOW MUCH ABOUT
Jack Kerouac

Born Jean-Louis Kerouac in the down-and-out manufacturing city of Lowell, Massachusetts, Jack Kerouac (1922–1969) was a central figure among the so-called Beat Generation of writers—in fact, he coined the term "Beat." In the 1950s, an era marked by conformity, the Beat writers believed in breaking the mold, and as writers they valued spontaneity and intuition, impulsiveness and free expression. Along with Allen Ginsberg's poem "Howl" (1956) and William S. Burroughs's novel *Naked Lunch* (1959), Kerouac's *On the Road* (1957)—a novel based on his cross-country road trip with his friend Neal Cassady—is considered one of the defining books of the Beat movement. Have you got the beat? Take this Kerouac quiz and see how you fare.

TRUE OR FALSE?

1. Kerouac was a star football player in high school.

2. Kerouac typed his *On the Road* manuscript on a single, 120-foot-long scroll of paper.

3. Kerouac spent seven years trying to find a publisher for *On the Road*.

4. English was not Kerouac's first language.

5. *The Dharma Bums* is based on Kerouac's travels with his fellow Beat poet Allen Ginsberg.

6. Kerouac was a vocal opponent of the Vietnam War.

ANSWERS

1. True. He attended Columbia University on a football scholarship.

2. True. He created the scroll so that his flow would not be interrupted by having to change typewriter paper.

3. True. Publishers told him again and again that the book was unpublishable.

4. True. Kerouac first learned joual, a dialect of French spoken in Quebec.

5. False. It's about a mountain-climbing trip that Kerouac took with Gary Snyder, the Zen poet known best for his nature poems.

6. False. Kerouac was politically conservative, and he supported the war in Vietnam.

DON'T KNOW MUCH ABOUT
James Joyce

"When you wet the bed first it is warm then it gets cold." It may be hard to believe that the man who wrote that sentence—from *A Portrait of the Artist as a Young Man* (1916)—also wrote *Ulysses* (1922) and *Finnegans Wake* (1939), two of the most infamously "difficult" works in the English language. James Joyce (d. 1941) was born in Dublin in 1882, and his middle-class, Catholic community would later inspire fiction like *Dubliners* (1914), the short-story collection that he called "a chapter of the moral history of my country." From the concise realism of *Dubliners*, Joyce's fiction moved toward experimental uses of language and stream-of-consciousness narration. Joyce's dense wordplay reaches a peak in *Finnegans Wake*, a work intended to be read aloud. If you're up for "a rhubarbarous maundarin yellagreen funkleblue wind-igut diodying" James Joyce quiz, read on!

1. What Joycean "holiday" do book lovers cele-brate on June 16?

2. What Christian term did Joyce borrow to de-scribe a "sudden spiritual moment" when "the soul of the commonest object" leaps out?

3. What is the name of Joyce's main character in *A Portrait of the Artist as a Young Man, Ulysses,* and the posthumously published fragment *Stephen Hero*?

4. What famed psychiatrist wrote to Joyce, "Your *Ulysses* has presented the world such an up-setting psychological problem, that repeat-edly I have been called in as a supposed authority on psychological matters"?

ANSWERS

1. In Dublin and many other cities June 16 is Bloomsday, named for the *Ulysses* character Leopold Bloom, and the day on which the entire book is set.

2. Epiphany.

3. Stephen Dedalus, inspired by the labyrinth builder of Greek myth.

4. Carl Jung. Joyce's daughter, Lucia, was treated by Jung.

DON'T KNOW MUCH ABOUT
Jorge Luis Borges

What if the world we know is only one of many parallel worlds, all existing at once? How do we know that we aren't just characters in somebody else's dream? If everyone believes in it, can a fictional world replace the real one? The Argentine writer Jorge Luis Borges (1899–1986) raised all these questions of metaphysics—the study of the nature of reality—in his mind-bending short stories. Fascinated with the idea of infinity, Borges imagined a point in space that contained all other points and perspectives (in the story "The Aleph"), as well as an immense library with books containing every possible combination of the alphabet, where works of genius and nonsense were shelved uselessly side by side (in "The Library of Babel"). Think you can navigate the labyrinth of Borges's life and work? Then take this quick quiz.

TRUE OR FALSE?

1. Borges never wrote a full-length novel.

2. Several Borges stories are reviews of novels that do not exist.

3. In one of Borges's most famous stories, a group of monkeys labor at typewriters, trying to re-create *Hamlet*.

4. In 1946 the newly elected president Juan Perón promoted Borges to the position of director of the National Library of Argentina.

ANSWERS

1. True. He claimed that he did not like novels and that he considered writing a long book "a laborious and impoverishing extravagance."

2. True. Most famous among these is "Pierre Menard, Author of the *Quixote*," a review of a book that seems to be identical to Cervantes's *Don Quixote*.

3. False.

4. False. Perón's government, suspicious of Borges's political writings, actually gave him a so-called promotion to the bureaucratic post of Inspector of Poultry and Rabbits in the Public Markets. Borges later did become director of the National Library, but he resigned after Perón's 1973 re-election.

DON'T KNOW MUCH ABOUT
Beowulf

*B*eowulf is a bloodbath. In this Anglo-Saxon epic, half rooted in Norse legend and half in sixth-century Danish history, monsters feast on sleeping warriors, and battle-tested swords melt in steaming blood and shatter against dragon scales. The hero Beowulf proves himself again and again in swordfights, hand-to-hand combat, and even underwater battles with beasts and dragons, making *Beowulf* one of the bloodiest books in high school English classrooms. For years, however, scholars treated the epic—probably written in the eighth century—more like a historical and linguistic source than a literary masterpiece. One of the first to argue that readers should value the gory and fantastic elements of *Beowulf* was the Oxford professor J. R. R. Tolkien, author of *The Lord of the Rings*.

In a 1936 lecture called "The Monsters and the Critics," he called *Beowulf*'s unknown author a great poet, not an overly imaginative historian. If you think you know Hrothgar from Hrunting, try this *Beowulf* quiz . . . so long as you don't faint at the sight of blood.

1. **What monster, a descendant of the biblical Cain, is the first slain by Beowulf?**

2. **What trophy does Beowulf take from that first fight?**

3. **Who must Beowulf fight in his second battle?**

4. **What 1971 novel tells a story parallel to *Beowulf*, but from a villain's perspective?**

5. **What is "Hrunting"?**

6. **Who is the only soldier to stand by Beowulf when, as an old man, he must face an angry, fire-breathing dragon?**

ANSWERS

1. Grendel.

2. Grendel's arm, or "claw" in some versions.

3. Grendel's mother, who takes back her son's claw and devours a Danish soldier in revenge for Grendel's death.

4. *Grendel,* by John Gardner.

5. Beowulf's sword.

6. Wiglaf.

DON'T KNOW MUCH ABOUT
The Pulitzer

First of all, say "PYOO-litzer." Okay, now you're ready to learn a little about this coveted American award. In accordance with the will of the Hungarian-born journalist-turned-publisher Joseph Pulitzer, these awards are decided in secret deliberations each year and are announced by the president of Columbia University in April. Although the number of prizes—not to mention the cash sum that comes with each one—has increased since the first were awarded in 1917, the main categories have remained the same: Journalism, Letters, Drama, and Music. Show off your winning knowledge with this Pulitzer Prize quiz.

1. **Who was the first woman to win a Pulitzer for a novel?**

2. Three playwrights have each won three or more Pulitzers for Drama. Who are they?

3. Hemingway's *For Whom the Bell Tolls* was nominated for the 1941 prize for a novel, but the judges that year chose not to award the prize at all. Which Hemingway novel did win twelve years later?

4. What graphic novel won a Special Citation in 1992, making it the only Pulitzer-winning comic book to date?

5. Why did Byron Price, director of the Office of Censorship, win a Special Award for Journalism in 1944?

6. What prize category, added in 1922, was first won by a work called "On the Road to Moscow"?

ANSWERS

1. Edith Wharton, for *The Age of Innocence* (1920), in 1921.

2. Eugene O'Neill (*Beyond the Horizon, Anna Christie, Strange Interlude, Long Day's Journey into Night*), Robert E. Sherwood (*Idiot's Delight, Abe Lincoln in Illinois, There Shall Be No Night*), and Edward Albee (*A Delicate Balance, Seascape, Three Tall Women*).

3. *The Old Man and the Sea* (in 1953).

4. *MAUS*, by Art Spiegelman.

5. For creating the newspaper and radio censorship codes.

6. Editorial cartoon. Rollin Kirby was the cartoonist.

DON'T KNOW MUCH ABOUT
More Fictional First Lines

"It was a dark and stormy night . . ."" Dying to know more? Edward George Bulwer-Lytton hoped you would be: he penned this now-clichéd opening for his novel *Paul Clifford* (1830). In his honor, the English Department at San Jose State University now holds the annual Bulwer-Lytton Fiction Contest, a competition in which writers submit the *worst* opening lines they can. The openers below might not get the Bulwer-Lytton nod, but see how many of the novels you can identify based on these first lines.

1. **You don't know about me, without you have read a book by the name of *The Adventures of Tom Sawyer*, but that ain't no matter. That book was made by Mr. Mark Twain, and he told the truth, mainly.**

2. Captain Ahab was neither my first husband nor my last.

3. It was a bright cold day in April, and the clocks were striking thirteen.

4. I was born in the city of Bombay . . . once upon a time. No, that won't do, there's no getting around the date: I was born in Doctor Narlikar's Nursing Home on August 15th, 1947.

5. The island of Gont, a single mountain that lifts its peak a mile above the storm-racked Northeast Sea, is a land famous for wizards.

ANSWERS

1. *Adventures of Huckleberry Finn*, by Mark Twain.

2. *Ahab's Wife*, by Sena Jeter Naslund.

3. *1984*, by George Orwell.

4. *Midnight's Children*, by Salman Rushdie.

5. *A Wizard of Earthsea*, by Ursula K. Le Guin.

DON'T KNOW MUCH ABOUT
Joseph Conrad

A steamer traveling up the Congo. An island in the South Seas. These were the settings not only for Joseph Conrad's dark and adventurous fiction, but also for the first half of his life. Born into the Polish nobility, Conrad (1857–1924) first apprenticed on a ship as a teenager, then spent twenty years working his way to master mariner. In his lifetime he was known best for his sea stories. But like Herman Melville, a seafaring author before him, Conrad was much more than an adventure writer. Marlow, Conrad's recurring narrator, is a keen observer of human nature, and books like *Heart of Darkness* (1902) and *Lord Jim* (1900) are intriguing psychological journeys. Have you seen "The horror! The horror!"? Journey into the heart of this Conrad quiz.

TRUE OR FALSE?

1. Conrad did not learn English until he was twenty-one years old.

2. Conrad lived for several months on the South Seas island of Patusan, where the novella *Lord Jim* is set.

3. Mr. Kurtz, the ivory trader in *Heart of Darkness*, was likely based on Leon Rom, a Belgian officer who kept severed heads in his garden plot.

4. The Nigerian novelist Chinua Achebe called Conrad a "bloody racist" in a controversial 1977 essay.

5. T. S. Eliot's long poem "The Waste Land" uses Mr. Kurtz's last words in *Heart of Darkness*—"The horror! The horror!"—as its epigraph.

ANSWERS

1. True. Conrad first learned English aboard a British merchant ship in 1878.

2. False. Patusan is not a real island.

3. True. For more on Rom, check out Adam Hochschild's excellent history, *King Leopold's Ghost.*

4. True. Achebe's essay, "An Image of Africa," called attention to the nonspeaking, dehumanized African characters in Conrad's work, especially the "savages" in *Heart of Darkness.* The essay was controversial because the novel had generally been praised for its critique of European colonialism in Africa.

5. False. Eliot intended to use the line as an epigraph, but Ezra Pound, who edited the poem, objected. The line was replaced with a quote by the Roman author Petronius.

DON'T KNOW MUCH ABOUT
Kurt Vonnegut

*The moral of the story is, is we're here on Earth
to fart around.*

Kurt Vonnegut Jr. (1922–2007) liked to remind his readers not to take life too seriously. In his novels, science fiction and social satire were never served up without a dose of black humor. If his fiction also ventured into the absurd, it's because Vonnegut thought that life itself was chaotic and irrational. *Slaughterhouse-Five* (1969) incorporated extraterrestrial life and time travel with real twentieth-century events, such as the 1945 firebombing of Dresden during World War II—which Vonnegut actually survived as a prisoner of war. If you know what "happened, more or less," take this quick quiz.

1. **What planet do the toilet-plunger-shaped aliens in *Slaughterhouse-Five* come from?**

2. What novel did Kurt Vonnegut write after witnessing machines replace machinists at General Electric (where Vonnegut worked in PR)?

3. In *Slaughterhouse-Five*, what famous phrase appears after every death?

4. Did Vonnegut actually begin an MIT commencement address with the advice, "Wear sunscreen"?

5. What recurring Vonnegut character writes dozens of science-fiction stories but can get them published only in pornographic magazines?

6. Besides *Slaughterhouse-Five*, which of his novels did Vonnegut grade an "A-plus"?

ANSWERS

1. Trafalmadore.

2. *Player Piano* (1952).

3. "So it goes."

4. No. This was a rumor that circulated widely on the Internet. The speech attributed to Vonnegut was actually a newspaper column by the *Chicago Tribune* writer Mary Schmich.

5. Kilgore Trout.

6. *Cat's Cradle* (1963).

DON'T KNOW MUCH ABOUT
Vladimir Nabokov

There's a lot more to Vladimir Nabokov (1899–1977) than *Lolita*. Born into extreme wealth in czarist Saint Petersburg, Nabokov fled Russia with his family in the wake of the Bolshevik Revolution. He published nine novels in Russian—his first language—before switching to English in the 1940s. Though his life was remarkable, and his other books like *Pale Fire* are considered classics, Nabokov's name is synonymous with *Lolita*, the story of Humbert Humbert, a middle-aged pedophile who has sex with his twelve-year-old stepdaughter. Scandal erupted when *Lolita* was first published in 1955—and was banned in France, though not in America. Some found the book repugnant, immoral, or pornographic, but others saw humor in *Lolita*, reading it as a parody of American culture, melodramatic romance stories, and Freudian analysis. Today *Lolita* is just as edgy and unsettling as it was in 1955. How much do you know about "that book by Nabokov"? Take this quiz and find out.

1. In what language was *Lolita* originally written?

2. What is Lolita's real name?

3. As the narrator Humbert Humbert writes his memoir from prison, he awaits trial for what crime?

4. What does Humbert Humbert call the young girls to whom he is so attracted?

5. Bonus question: What children's story, whose author had a controversial obsession with young girls, did Nabokov translate into Russian?

6. What was Nabokov's other profession?

ANSWERS

1. English. *Lolita* was first published in France, though, because at first no American publisher would touch it. It became a bestseller in 1955.

2. Dolores Haze.

3. Murder.

4. Nymphets.

5. *Alice's Adventures in Wonderland*, by Lewis Carroll.

6. Nabokov also taught entomology at Harvard and discovered several new species of butterfly, including "Nabokov's wood nymph."

DON'T KNOW MUCH ABOUT
Nathaniel Hawthorne

Nathaniel Hawthorne's preoccupation with sin, guilt, intolerance, and hypocrisy in Puritan America began at home: his own ancestors, who arrived in Massachusetts as early as 1630, fought against Indians, persecuted Quakers, and sat as judges in the Salem witchcraft trials. Fascinated by this dark family history, Hawthorne (1804–1864) put colonial Puritan communities at the center of his best-known works, including *Twice-Told Tales* (1837) and *The Scarlet Letter* (1850). Hawthorne's Hester Prynne, who displays an embroidered letter "A" across her breast as punishment for adultery—enduring shame and ostracism, and wearing her sin for all to see—stands as one of the best-loved heroines in American literature. Of course you'd never tell who Hester's secret lover was, but see if you can answer these other Hawthorne quiz questions.

1. What real-life experiment in communal living inspired the novel *The Blithedale Romance* (1852)?

2. Which twentieth-century author wrote a trilogy of novels, beginning with *A Month of Sundays* (1975), based on *The Scarlet Letter*?

3. In Hawthorne's short story "Young Goodman Brown," who does the title character go to the woods to meet?

4. What Hawthorne novel, spanning many years, contains the moral that "the wrong-doing of one generation lives into the successive ones"?

ANSWERS

1. Brook Farm, a transcendentalist community outside Boston.

2. John Updike. The other novels are *S.* and *Roger's Version.*

3. The devil.

4. *The House of the Seven Gables.*

DON'T KNOW MUCH ABOUT
The Thousand and One Nights

Could you tell a good story if your life depended on it? Scheherazade sure could. In the classic *The Thousand and One Nights* (sometimes published as *The Arabian Nights*), a king takes a bride each night and has her murdered in the morning. But Scheherazade, his clever new wife, has a plan: early each morning she begins a story but doesn't finish telling it. Day after day, the king spares her life so that he can hear the ending—talk about a cliff-hanger! The story of Scheherazade and the king is what's called a "frame narrative"—a vehicle for countless other tales—and the first known manuscripts, which date from the fourteenth century, combine Persian, Arab, Indian, and Egyptian lore. Over the years, now-familiar tales like those of Aladdin, Sinbad the Sailor, and Ali Baba were incorporated into the frame. Now say "Open Sesame!" and see if you can crack this quick quiz.

TRUE OR FALSE?

1. **There are exactly one thousand stories in the definitive edition of *The Thousand and One Nights*.**

2. **The tales most familiar to Western audiences—those of Aladdin and Ali Baba—were added by the first European translator of the work.**

3. **Many of the genies in the *Nights* are mean and threatening—not the friendly wish-granters of Disney's *Aladdin* or television's *I Dream of Jeannie*.**

4. **In Edgar Allan Poe's story "The Thousand-and-Second Tale of Scheherazade," Scheherazade begins telling the story of *The Thousand and One Nights*, creating an infinite loop of the same story-within-a-story.**

ANSWERS

1. False. There is no "definitive" text or translation of the *Nights*, but most contain well under one thousand tales.

2. True. Antoine Galland, who first translated the *Nights* into French in the early 1700s, added these tales. Their origin is unclear, and some scholars contend that Galland invented the stories himself.

3. True. Genies can be good or evil, and often the wishes they grant lead to unintended misfortune.

4. False. The never-ending *Nights* loop is a detail of Jorge Luis Borges's "The Garden of Forking Paths." In Poe's story, Scheherazade tells the king about nineteenth-century technology—and he executes her for telling such an over-the-top fiction.

DON'T KNOW MUCH ABOUT
Salman Rushdie

A Million Little Pieces. Lolita. The Anarchist Cookbook. Lots of books are considered controversial, but few lead to death threats. When Salman Rushdie's *The Satanic Verses* hit bookstores in 1988, the author was forced to go into hiding—for nine years. Iran's spiritual leader, Ayatollah Khomeini, deemed the book an insult to Islam and declared a fatwa, or religious edict, calling on Muslims to execute Rushdie (b. 1947). At the heart of this firestorm were two dreams of Gibreel Farishta, a fictional movie star who, after surviving a plane crash, imagines that he is the Archangel Gabriel. In one of them, Gibreel dreams of a brothel where the prostitutes adopt the names of the prophet Muhammad's wives. Only in 1998 did the Iranian foreign minister finally drop the official death threat against Rushdie. Though *The Satanic Verses* made more headlines than most books, there's much more to Salman Rushdie and his writing. See how much of it you know in this quick quiz.

1. While he was in hiding, what children's book did Rushdie write for his son Zafar?

2. In Rushdie's Booker Prize–winning novel *Midnight's Children* (1981), 1001 children are born with magical powers at midnight on the day of what historical event?

3. What Greek myth inspired the plot of *The Ground Beneath Her Feet* (1999)?

4. What honor did Rushdie achieve in 2008?

ANSWERS

1. *Haroun and the Sea of Stories* (1990).

2. India's independence from British rule, August 15, 1947. The previous day, British India had been partitioned into secular India and Muslim Pakistan.

3. The myth of Orpheus and Eurydice, about a musician who follows his dead wife into the underworld.

4. *Midnight's Children* was selected as the winner of the Best of the Booker award. Readers around the world voted the 1981 novel as the best of the prestigious prize winners.

DON'T KNOW MUCH ABOUT
T. S. Eliot

Weialala leia. Twit twit twit. O O O O. Goonight. Goonight. As if the Latin, Greek, and Sanskrit weren't enough, T. S. Eliot (1886–1965) rounds out the voices in "The Waste Land" with music and bird-song and drunken good-byes. The 1922 poem, about a barren civilization in need of spiritual renewal, is incredibly challenging because of its medley of languages and obscure literary references. Eliot actually wanted "The Waste Land" to be difficult—only complex poetry, he felt, could match "the immense panorama of futility and anarchy which is contemporary history." Seeking new cultural life in the intellectual and religious traditions of Europe, the American-born poet transplanted himself there. "Do you dare" take this quick T. S. Eliot quiz? Read on.

1. Whose poetry did Eliot call "the most persistent and deepest influence on my verse"?

2. The opening lines of "The Waste Land"—"April is the cruellest month . . ."—are a pessimistic twist on the beginning of which classic poem?

3. Which fellow poet heavily edited "The Waste Land"?

4. Which T. S. Eliot poem contains the famous lines, "Do I dare / Disturb the universe?"

5. What country granted Eliot citizenship in 1927?

ANSWERS

1. Dante.

2. The General Prologue of *The Canterbury Tales* by Geoffrey Chaucer.

3. Ezra Pound. In the poem, Eliot acknowledges Pound as "*il miglior fabbro*," or "the better maker."

4. "The Love Song of J. Alfred Prufrock" (1917).

5. Great Britain. That year, Eliot also became a member of the Church of England.

DON'T KNOW MUCH ABOUT
Victor Hugo

"One can resist the invasion of armies," wrote Victor Hugo; "one cannot resist the invasion of ideas." The poet, novelist, and playwright Victor-Marie Hugo (1802–1885) served as a politician in three separate French governments, but he felt that his greatest contribution to humanity could be made through literature. He imagined that *Les Misérables* (1862) would be a revolutionary novel, stirring readers toward compassion and justice. It told the story of Jean Valjean, an ex-convict who tries to redeem himself in an unforgiving society. But like Hugo's *The Hunchback of Notre-Dame* (1831), the novel is best known now for its stage and screen reincarnations. How much do you know about these Hugo-inspired dramas?

TRUE OR FALSE?

1. Hugo adapted both *The Hunchback of Notre-Dame* and *Les Misérables* for the stage.

2. The first film adaptation of *The Hunchback of Notre-Dame* was made by Alice Guy-Blaché—the first woman film director.

3. Giuseppe Verdi based his operas *Rigoletto* and *Ernani* on Hugo plays.

4. Literary critics hailed the 1996 Disney cartoon version of *The Hunchback of Notre-Dame* for following Hugo's novel so closely.

5. *Les Misérables* was filmed as a movie many times before it was transformed into a musical.

6. The François Truffaut film *L'histoire d'Adèle H.* (1975) is about Victor Hugo's wife.

ANSWERS

1. False. Hugo wrote many plays, but he did not adapt his novels.

2. True. The 1905 film was called *La Esméralda*.

3. True. The plays are *Le roi s'amuse* (1832) and *Hernani* (1830).

4. False. Hugo's novel is much darker; it does not have the happy Disney ending.

5. True. The wildly successful musical adaptation did not appear onstage until the 1980s.

6. False. The "Adèle H." of the title is Hugo's daughter, whom he put in a mental institution.

DON'T KNOW MUCH ABOUT
Toni Morrison

In her 1993 Nobel Prize lecture, Toni Morrison (b. 1931) called language an "act with consequences." Her writing has consistently reckoned with the power of language—the power to repress and to do violence, but also the power to create meaning out of diverse experiences. Morrison's fictional debut came in 1970 with *The Bluest Eye*, a novel about a troubled girl in Lorain, Ohio—Morrison's hometown—who is raped by her father. Subsequent novels, including *Beloved*, *Sula*, and *Paradise*, have been equally unflinching. On a parallel track to her successful fiction career, Morrison has been an influential academic. In *Playing in the Dark* (1992), she argued that much of the great American literature hailed as "universal" deals with the experience of being white. If Morrison's books are beloved to you, take this quiz to see how much you really know about the author.

1. **What is Toni Morrison's real name?**

2. **What does Pecola Breedlove, the young heroine of *The Bluest Eye*, wish for?**

3. **In *Beloved*, why does Sethe cut her daughter's throat?**

4. **Who starred as Sethe in the film version of *Beloved*?**

5. **Which Morrison novel received the Pulitzer Prize in 1988?**

6. **Which Morrison novel takes its title from one of the raciest sections of the Bible?**

7. **Which two Morrison novels were among the "Most Frequently Challenged" books—those that receive the most requests for removal from school and library shelves—in 2006?**

8. **What Morrison-inspired memorial was dedicated in 2008?**

ANSWERS

1. Chloe Anthony Wofford. Morrison has claimed that she regrets taking on the pen name.

2. Blue eyes, which she thinks will make her more loved.

3. So she will not grow up in slavery.

4. Oprah Winfrey. Four of Morrison's books—*Sula, The Bluest Eye, Paradise,* and *Song of Solomon*—have been Oprah's Book Club selections.

5. *Beloved.*

6. *Song of Solomon.*

7. *The Bluest Eye* and *Beloved,* for both sexual content and offensive language.

8. A "bench by the road" near Charleston, South Carolina. Morrison once said that America lacked any memorials to slavery, not even a "bench by the road."

DON'T KNOW MUCH ABOUT
Short Story First Lines

"Brevity is the soul of lingerie," Dorothy Parker once said. That may be true, but it's also the soul of great short stories. Every word counts, which may explain why so many good ones have great opening lines. To keep this brief, which of these short stories can you identify by their first lines?

1. True!—nervous—very, very dreadfully nervous I had been and am; but why *will* you say that I am mad?

2. None of them knew the color of the sky.

3. In walks these three girls in nothing but bathing suits.

4. One dollar and eighty-seven cents. That was all. And sixty cents of it was in pennies.

5. Lily, the caretaker's daughter, was literally run off her feet.

ANSWERS

1. "The Tell-Tale Heart," by Edgar Allan Poe.

2. "The Open Boat," by Stephen Crane.

3. "A & P," by John Updike.

4. "The Gift of the Magi," by O. Henry.

5. "The Dead," by James Joyce.

DON'T KNOW MUCH ABOUT
Villains

S ome literary bad guys you can't help but love a little, while others you just love to hate. How many of these unctuous, infamous, demonic, obsequious, dastardly, and just plain evil characters in fiction can you name? Bonus points for title and author.

1. **This orphan returns to his adoptive home a rich man, and there he wreaks physical and psychological vengeance on the families who spurned him.**

2. **This monster crawls from a murky lake to feed on Danish warriors; once he is killed, his mother avenges his death.**

3. The cruel sister of David Copperfield's step-mother, she is the "confidential friend" of David's wife Dora Spenlow.

4. This twisted character changes his last name from "Prynne" to something tellingly cold-sounding in order to avoid association with his adulterous wife.

5. Though he was christened Tom Marvolo Riddle, this villain is so feared that none dare speak his name.

6. This brilliant psychiatrist has an insatiable appetite for something unspeakable.

7. This cruel plantation owner tries to break slaves of their religious beliefs.

8. An obsessed police officer, this character eventually throws himself into the River Seine.

9. This impulsive, lusty beast is the alter ego of a mild-mannered scientist.

ANSWERS

1. Heathcliff, in Emily Brontë's *Wuthering Heights*.

2. Grendel, in *Beowulf.*

3. Miss Jane Murdstone, in Charles Dickens's *David Copperfield*.

4. Roger Chillingworth, in Nathaniel Hawthorne's *The Scarlet Letter*.

5. Lord Voldemort, in J. K. Rowling's *Harry Potter* series.

6. The cannibalistic Hannibal Lecter, in Thomas Harris's *Red Dragon, The Silence of the Lambs,* and *Hannibal Rising.*

7. Simon Legree, in Harriet Beecher Stowe's *Uncle Tom's Cabin*.

8. Inspector Javert, in Victor Hugo's *Les Misérables*.

9. Mr. Hyde, in Robert Louis Stevenson's *The Strange Case of Dr. Jekyll and Mr. Hyde.*

DON'T KNOW MUCH ABOUT
William Butler Yeats

As Ireland struggled for independence in the early twentieth century, a group of poets and playwrights began a movement known as the Irish Literary Revival. Leading them was William Butler Yeats (1865–1939), a poet and playwright who wanted "to create a whole literature, a whole dramatic movement" from the epics of Celtic legend and the folklore, fairy tales, and ballads of his native Ireland. Though Yeats served in the first Irish Senate in 1922, his lyrical poetry often kept its distance from politics: in "The Lake Isle of Innisfree" (1893), for example, the poet yearns for a peaceful escape, while in later poems, like "Politics" (1939), he would rather pay attention to a pretty girl than to "war and war's alarms." Now "Come away, O human child!" and see how you fare on this W. B. Yeats quiz.

1. Could Yeats speak Gaelic?

2. Which nationalistic Yeats play premiered with his unrequited love, Maud Gonne, playing the title role?

3. Which hero of Irish legend, sometimes called the "Irish Achilles," was featured in five Yeats plays?

4. Which Yeats poem eulogizes the Irish patriots killed in the 1916 Easter Rising and expresses his ambivalence about militant nationalism with the line, "A terrible beauty is born"?

5. In which poem, written in the aftermath of World War I, does the poet warn of a political situation in which "Things fall apart; the centre cannot hold"?

6. Which Yeats myth re-creates a scene from Greek mythology, imagining the violent history that will follow from a young woman's rape by Zeus?

ANSWERS

1. No. Yeats believed in reviving the Irish language, but he never succeeded in learning to speak or read it himself.

2. *Cathleen ni Houlihan* (1902).

3. Cuchulain (pronounced *koo-hool-n*).

4. "Easter, 1916" (1916).

5. "The Second Coming" (1919).

6. "Leda and the Swan" (1928).

DON'T KNOW MUCH ABOUT
William Faulkner

The past is never dead. It's not even past.

History haunts the present in William Faulkner's novels, as this famous line from *Requiem for a Nun* (1951) suggests. Faulkner (1897–1962) was born in Mississippi, and his great novels focus on the decline of the Southern aristocracy in and around the fictional town of Jefferson. He invented old Mississippi families like the Compsons, the Bundrens, the Sutpens, and the McCaslins in such novels as *The Sound and the Fury* (1929), *As I Lay Dying* (1930), and *Absalom, Absalom!* (1936), as well as in interrelated short stories like those in *Go Down, Moses* (1942). Eventually recognized with the Nobel Prize in 1949, Faulkner couldn't pay the bills with his fiction. Like many writers of his day, Faulkner went west, seeking income as a Hollywood screenwriter. Think you know this American literary master? Take this quick quiz and find out.

1. In what fictional county is most of Faulkner's Mississippi fiction set?

2. Which mentally retarded character narrates the first section of *The Sound and the Fury*?

3. Which Faulkner masterpiece takes its title from a biblical passage in which King David mourns his dead son?

4. Which Faulkner novel features Joe Christmas, an orphan who wants to know his racial lineage?

5. Which movie, starring Humphrey Bogart and Lauren Bacall, had a screenplay adapted by William Faulkner from a novel by Ernest Hemingway?

ANSWERS

1. Yoknapatawpha County.

2. Benjy Compson.

3. *Absalom, Absalom!*

4. *Light in August* (1932).

5. *To Have and Have Not* (1944). Faulkner also adapted Raymond Chandler's novel *The Big Sleep* for the 1946 Bogart and Bacall movie of the same name.

DON'T KNOW MUCH ABOUT
F. Scott Fitzgerald

"It was an age of miracles, it was an age of art, it was an age of excess, and it was an age of satire." In his work and his life, F. Scott Fitzgerald (1896–1940) captured the spirit of the Roaring Twenties. Against a backdrop of bright lights, jazz, and liquor (lots of liquor), such novels as *This Side of Paradise* (1920) and *The Great Gatsby* (1925) follow Fitzgerald's bright-eyed protagonists as they chase the American Dream—usually to disillusionment. In the early 1920s, Fitzgerald's life seemed charmed: his novels brought financial success, he married his Southern belle sweetheart Zelda Sayre, and the couple soon had a daughter. But by the end of the decade, everything crashed. Fitzgerald drank more and more heavily, his income could not pay for the family's decadent lifestyle, and in 1930, Zelda checked into a sanatorium during the first of many breakdowns. Fitzgerald died of a heart attack in Hollywood, where he was struggling as a screenwriter, in 1940. If you think you know what's great about Gatsby, take this quiz about Fitzgerald's fiction.

1. What novel, originally titled *The Romantic Egoist*, made Fitzgerald a celebrity practically overnight?

2. What phrase, frequently used to describe the 1920s, is Fitzgerald credited with coining?

3. What 1922 Fitzgerald novel fictionalized the romance between F. Scott and Zelda Sayre Fitzgerald?

4. In the *Great Gatsby*, what is the name of the East Egg socialite whom Jay Gatsby longs for?

5. Which novel infuriated Zelda Fitzgerald with its depiction of Nicole Diver's mental breakdown?

ANSWERS

1. *This Side of Paradise*, his first book.

2. "The Jazz Age." Fitzgerald published a story collection called *Tales of the Jazz Age* in 1922.

3. *The Beautiful and Damned*.

4. Daisy Buchanan.

5. *Tender Is the Night*.

DON'T KNOW MUCH ABOUT
Langston Hughes

As a young man, Langston Hughes (1902–1967) stated a mission for his generation of black writers: "to express our individual dark-skinned selves without fear or shame." He wrote "The Negro Speaks of Rivers," his first published poem, shortly after graduating from high school in 1920, and a few years later he became a central figure in the Harlem Renaissance. Hughes gained prominence for writing poetry inspired by blues and jazz music; his first collection was called *The Weary Blues* (1926). Prolific as a poet, he also wrote plays, short stories, novels, newspaper sketches, essays, and two autobiographies. How much do you know about the "poet laureate of Harlem"? Take this quick quiz and see.

1. With which fellow Harlem Renaissance author did Hughes cowrite the play *Mule Bone*?

2. Which character, originally from Hughes's newspaper columns, sits on a barstool in Harlem delivering social commentary?

3. In a description of himself written for a biographical dictionary, which three poets did Hughes call his "chief influences"?

4. From what language did Hughes translate other poets' work into English?

5. What European city did Hughes visit in 1933 in order to film a movie about African American life in the United States?

ANSWERS

1. Zora Neale Hurston. Hughes and Hurston co-wrote *Mule Bone* in 1930, but because of a falling out, it was not produced until after both their deaths.

2. James B. Semple, or "Simple."

3. Paul Laurence Dunbar, Carl Sandburg, and Walt Whitman.

4. Spanish. Some of the poets he translated are Gabriela Mistral, Nicolás Guillén, and Federico García Lorca.

5. Moscow. The film was never made, perhaps on account of its far-fetched plot: black steelworkers in Alabama are rescued from their plight by a team of white union members and Red Army soldiers.

DON'T KNOW MUCH ABOUT
Nobel Prize Winners (and Losers)

The supreme international literary honor, the Nobel Prize in Literature goes to the living author who has "produced in the field of literature the most outstanding work in an ideal direction," as the prize founder Alfred Nobel stated in his will. Over the years, however, the Swedish Academy for the Nobel Prize has not always picked a crowd-pleaser to win this *crème de la crème* award. Earn your own laurels by identifying which of these great twentieth-century writers wore the coveted medallion of the Nobel laureate in Literature . . . and which ones were overlooked by the Nobel nod.

1. **James Joyce**

2. **Gabriel García Márquez**

3. Franz Kafka

4. Gertrude Stein

5. Kurt Vonnegut

6. John Steinbeck

7. Ernest Hemingway

8. Hermann Hesse

9. Willa Cather

10. Jean-Paul Sartre

11. Virginia Woolf

ANSWERS

1. The author of what many consider the "greatest novel," *Ulysses*, never won.

2. The author of *One Hundred Years of Solitude* won in 1982.

3. Never won.

4. Never won.

5. Never won.

6. Won in 1962.

7. Won in 1954.

8. Won in 1946.

9. Never won.

10. Won in 1964.

11. Never won.

DON'T KNOW MUCH ABOUT
The Literature of War

"War is at best barbarism," the Civil War general William T. Sherman once said; "its glory is all moonshine." Some of the most eloquent voices in literature have emerged from their war experience, exploring that "barbarism"—the darkest corners of human nature—and attempting to describe the unspeakable with words. See if you can identify these poets and novelists, all of them soldiers or combat veterans.

1. Probably the best-known poet of World War I, this Englishman wrote "Anthem for Doomed Youth" and "Dulce et Decorum Est." He was killed one week before the armistice was declared in 1918.

2. In 1932 this author fled Nazi Germany, where copies of his novel about the horrors of World War I were burned in public bonfires.

3. This author's most famous novel is based on his experience of the Dresden firebombing during World War II.

4. This author, a B-25 bombardier during World War II, wrote his greatest novel about the question, "What does a sane man do in an insane society?"

5. Though opposed to the Vietnam War, this author reported for duty; he served as an infantry foot soldier in the American division involved in the 1968 My Lai massacre.

ANSWERS

1. Wilfred Owen.

2. Erich Maria Remarque, author of *All Quiet on the Western Front.*

3. Kurt Vonnegut, author of *Slaughterhouse-Five,* who was in Dresden as a POW during the air attack.

4. Joseph Heller, author of *Catch-22.*

5. Tim O'Brien.

DON'T KNOW MUCH ABOUT
John Keats

Imagine writing one great ode: a lofty, lyrical poem that could soar to the heights of rhapsody in one stanza and plunge to the depths of mortal suffering in the next. Well, John Keats wrote six of them. In less than a year. When he was only twenty-four years old. Between 1818 and 1819, a furiously imaginative period known as his annus mirabilis (year of wonders), Keats lost his brother to tuberculosis and fell head-over-heels in love. He also produced dozens of poems, including two versions of the epic *Hyperion* and his six major odes. Five of these he wrote in a three-and-a-half-week burst between April and May 1819: "Ode to Psyche," "Ode on a Grecian Urn," "Ode to a Nightingale," "Ode on Melancholy," and "Ode on Indolence." He completed the sequence that September with a mournful celebration of fleeting splendor, "To Autumn." In "Ode on a Grecian Urn," Keats wrote the famous line, "Beauty is truth, truth beauty." See if you can separate the beautiful from the false in this quiz about Keats.

TRUE OR FALSE?

1. John Keats was born into one of London's wealthiest families.

2. Keats was barely five feet tall.

3. Childhood friends remembered Keats as a well-behaved, studious boy.

4. Ever a romantic, Keats's dying wish was that his name not appear on his grave.

5. Though his poetic output was prolific, Keats lived only to age twenty-five.

ANSWERS

1. False. Keats's family ran a London stable called the Swan and Hoop.

2. True. He once wrote, "My mind has been the most discontented and restless one that ever was put into a body too small for it."

3. False. Keats fought often as a boy; one school-mate recalled his "terrier courage."

4. True. His tombstone reads, "Here lies one whose name was writ in water."

5. True. Keats, born 1795, died from tuberculosis in 1821.

DON'T KNOW MUCH ABOUT
The Brontë Sisters

As children, the literary sisters Charlotte, Emily, and Anne Brontë, along with their brother Branwell, created fantasy kingdoms with names like "Gondal" and "Angria" and made them the settings for elaborate, ongoing poems and stories. This "juvenilia"—a fancy term for the work that artists produce in their younger years—provides evidence of a remarkably imaginative family, though the sisters took their youthful creativity in different directions, and Branwell fell into alcoholism. Charlotte (1816–1855) left behind the Angria sagas for the realism of *Jane Eyre* (1847). Anne (1820–1849) published semiautobiographical fiction like *Agnes Grey* (1847). And middle sister Emily (1818–1848) drew on the melodramas of Gondal and Angria to create the tempestuous novel *Wuthering Heights* (also 1847!).

How much do you know about this trio of Victorian writers? Take this quiz and find out.

1. None of the Brontë sisters—nor their brother nor two older sisters—lived to the age of forty. What disease killed all of them?

2. What job, considered respectable employment for middle-class Victorian women, do the title characters of Anne's *Agnes Grey* and Charlotte's *Jane Eyre* hold?

3. Which sister published a fictional account of her brother Branwell's alcoholism?

4. Which two characters fall passionately (and destructively) in love in Emily's *Wuthering Heights*?

5. Which Brontë novel begins with the line, "There was no possibility of taking a walk that day"?

6. What novel did Jean Rhys write as a prequel to *Jane Eyre*?

ANSWERS

1. Tuberculosis (known in their day as "consumption"). Charlotte's death may have been hastened by complications of pregnancy.

2. Governess.

3. Anne Brontë. The novel is *The Tenant of Wildfell Hall* (1848).

4. Catherine Earnshaw and Heathcliff.

5. *Jane Eyre*, by Charlotte Brontë.

6. *Wide Sargasso Sea* (1966).

DON'T KNOW MUCH ABOUT
More Poetic First Lines

"Gather ye rose-buds while ye may," wrote Robert Herrick, the seventeenth-century English poet, to open a poem encouraging ladies to marry while they were young and beautiful ("To the Virgins, to Make Much of Time"). This line of Herrick's poem, which gained popularity as a song, is now an iconic admonition to enjoy our lives. Now gather ye wits, and see how many of these famous first lines you can identify.

1. Something there is that doesn't love a wall

2. I, too, dislike it: there are things that are important beyond all this fiddle.

3. Bent double, like old beggars under sacks

4. By the rude bridge that arched the flood

5. Come live with me and be my love

6. God moves in a mysterious way

7. Hog Butcher for the World

8. Little Lamb, who made thee?

9. The art of losing isn't hard to master.

ANSWERS

1. Robert Frost, "Mending Wall."

2. Marianne Moore, "Poetry."

3. Wilfred Owen, "Dulce et Decorum Est."

4. Ralph Waldo Emerson, "Concord Hymn."

5. Christopher Marlowe, "The Passionate Shepherd to His Love."

6. William Cowper, "Light Shining Out of Darkness."

7. Carl Sandburg, "Chicago."

8. William Blake, "The Lamb."

9. Elizabeth Bishop, "One Art."

DON'T KNOW MUCH ABOUT
Catchy Titles

"Neither a borrower nor a lender be" was oft-repeated advice from Polonius in Shakespeare's *Hamlet*. But many writers have borrowed phrases from the Bard—and from dozens of other literary sources—with great success. How many of the titles below, all phrases on loan from prior literary works, can you identify?

1. *Tender Is the Night*, by F. Scott Fitzgerald

2. *A Raisin in the Sun*, by Lorraine Hansberry

3. *For Whom the Bell Tolls*, by Ernest Hemingway

4. *The Sound and the Fury*, by William Faulkner

5. *No Country for Old Men*, by Cormac McCarthy

6. *Where Angels Fear to Tread*, by E. M. Forster

7. *I Know Why the Caged Bird Sings*, by Maya Angelou

8. *The House of Mirth*, by Edith Wharton

ANSWERS

1. John Keats's poem "Ode to a Nightingale."

2. Langston Hughes's poem "Harlem."

3. John Donne's "Meditation XVII," from *Devotions upon Emergent Occasions*.

4. Shakespeare, *Macbeth*.

5. W. B. Yeats's poem "Sailing to Byzantium."

6. Alexander Pope, who wrote in *An Essay on Criticism*, "For fools rush in where angels fear to tread."

7. Paul Laurence Dunbar's poem "Sympathy."

8. The Bible (Ecclesiastes 7:4): "The heart of the wise is in the house of mourning; but the heart of fools is in the house of mirth."

DON'T KNOW MUCH ABOUT
Virginia Woolf

"Who's afraid of Virginia Woolf?" asks the title of Edward Albee's Pulitzer Prize–winning play. And generations of students have answered, "Me." But for many other readers, Virginia Woolf is both a beguiling voice and a fascinating character in her own right. Rejecting tidy storytelling conventions, the British author Virginia Woolf (1882–1941) set out to describe experience with words, experimenting with stream-of-consciousness narration to get inside her characters' minds. Woolf also played with the flow of time. In *Mrs. Dalloway* (1925), the clock of Big Ben chimes out the time while Clarissa Dalloway prepares for an evening party. Beneath the surface of Clarissa's consciousness, Woolf's long, winding sentences convey a slowed, internal time. Are you afraid of Virginia Woolf? Try this quick quiz.

1. To what literary circle did Virginia Woolf, her sister Vanessa, and both of their husbands belong?

2. What is the name of Woolf's hypothetical writer in *A Room of One's Own*, a woman denied opportunities?

3. In *Mrs. Dalloway*, what affliction does Clarissa Dalloway's friend Septimus Smith suffer from, as a result of his wartime experiences?

4. Before she committed suicide by drowning in 1941, Virginia and her husband Leonard Woolf made preparations for suicide in the event of what?

5. Who played Virginia Woolf in the film *The Hours* (based on the book by Michael Cunningham)?

ANSWERS

1. The Bloomsbury group, named for the London neighborhood.

2. Judith Shakespeare.

3. Shell shock. Now called "post-traumatic stress disorder," the syndrome figured prominently in the literature of the 1920s, as modernist writers tried to give literary form to this shattering psychological experience.

4. A Nazi invasion of Britain.

5. Nicole Kidman in an Oscar- and Golden Globe–winning performance.

DON'T KNOW MUCH ABOUT
V. S. Naipaul

"I don't stand for any country," V. S. Naipaul (b. 1932) told the media upon learning that he had won the Nobel Prize in 2001. The idea of being without a home or country—and as a result, constantly searching for an identity—runs through Naipaul's writing. Critics categorize Naipaul as a "postcolonial" writer, in part because he was born in Trinidad to Indian parents and writes about that country and other once-colonized places, but also because his work deals with the consequences of colonization: political and cultural confusion, or in his words, a world that is "mixed and secondhand." A controversial author, Naipaul has been embraced by some—even knighted by Queen Elizabeth!—but has drawn criticism from fellow writers like the West Indian Derek Walcott, the 1992 Nobel laureate; and the Nigerian Chinua Achebe, because he is so pessimistic about the futures of formerly colonized nations. What do you know about this man without a country? Take this quick quiz.

1. Who inspired the title character in *A House for Mr. Biswas* (1961)?

2. What book earned Naipaul the Booker Prize in 1971?

3. What religion was the subject of *Among the Believers* (1981) and *Beyond Belief* (1998)?

4. Where did Naipaul attend college?

5. How did Naipaul's Indian grandparents come to Trinidad?

ANSWERS

1. Seepersad Naipaul, V. S. Naipaul's father.

2. *In a Free State.*

3. Islam. Naipaul is a harsh critic of Islamic fundamentalism. One of his more inflammatory comments on the subject was that Islamic women in the West should not wear headscarves.

4. Oxford University. He left for England to attend school when he was eighteen, and he has lived there ever since.

5. They came as indentured servants—owing five years of labor in sugarcane fields to pay their passage from India.

DON'T KNOW MUCH ABOUT
Zora Neale Hurston

Zora Neale Hurston (1891?–1960) was a great storyteller—so great, in fact, that at age twenty-six, in order to finish high school, she claimed that she was only sixteen. For the rest of her life, Hurston maintained that she was at least ten years younger than she actually was—and always got away with it. Born in Alabama, Hurston grew up in Eatonville, Florida, the country's first incorporated all-black township and the setting for much of her fiction, including the masterpiece *Their Eyes Were Watching God* (1937). Eatonville was, she wrote, "a city of five lakes, three croquet courts, three hundred brown skins, three hundred good swimmers, plenty guavas, two schools, and no jailhouse." Hurston relocated to New York City in 1925, where fellow Harlem Renaissance writers embraced her dynamic, life-of-the-party personality and her writing: collections of folklore as well as her fiction, which combined rich, figurative language with Hurston's remarkable ear for dialect. Take this Zora Neale Hurston quiz and see if you should check out *Dust Tracks on a Road* (1942), her autobiography.

TRUE OR FALSE?

1. Zora Neale Hurston studied at Barnard University, where she was the school's first African American student.

2. *Their Eyes Were Watching God* was controversial because it depicted a black woman "passing" in white society.

3. Hurston traveled to Africa to research folklore and collect stories.

4. Zora Neale Hurston's grave remained unmarked until 1973, when a young writer named Alice Walker journeyed to Florida to place a gravestone there.

ANSWERS

1. True. Hurston graduated from Barnard in 1928 after studying anthropology under the Columbia professor Franz Boas, renowned as the father of American anthropology.

2. False. *Their Eyes Were Watching God*, which features the fiercely independent Janie, is set in all-black communities like Eatonville and features almost no white characters. Nella Larsen's *Passing* is the story of a black woman "passing" as white.

3. False. Hurston's ethnographic fieldwork did, however, take her through the American South, Haiti, and Jamaica.

4. True. The author of *The Color Purple*, Walker described this experience in a 1975 piece for *Ms.* magazine, "In Search of Zora Neale Hurston."

DON'T KNOW MUCH ABOUT
Poetic Last Lines

"Nevermore!" It might be difficult to end a poem on a more dramatic note than Edgar Allan Poe did in "The Raven." Can you name the poets who created these ending lines? Bonus points for the name of the poem.

1. Till human voices wake us, and we drown.

2. My soul has grown deep like the rivers.

3. and so cold

4. And eternity in an hour

5. Petals on a wet, black bough.

6. Daddy, daddy, you bastard, I'm through.

ANSWERS

1. T. S. Eliot, "The Love Song of J. Alfred Pru-frock."

2. Langston Hughes, "The Negro Speaks of Rivers."

3. William Carlos Williams, "This Is Just to Say."

4. William Blake, "To see a world in a grain of sand."

5. Ezra Pound, "In a Station of the Metro."

6. Sylvia Plath, "Daddy."

DON'T KNOW MUCH ABOUT
Epitaphs

An "epitaph" is the inscription on a gravestone (not to be confused with an "epigraph," or quotation at the beginning of a book or poem). The word comes from the Greek phrase meaning "over a tomb," and it once referred to the words spoken during funeral rites. Epitaphs can be witty or sentimental, and many caution the reader about his or her own mortality. In seventeenth-century England, the epitaph even rose to prominence as a genre of poetry—though these epitaphs, by poets like Ben Jonson and John Donne, were not necessarily inscribed on graves. Know which words mark your favorite author's final resting place? Take this quiz and see how many epitaphs you can identify.

1. Which writer is buried beneath these lines from her own novel: ". . . that is happiness; to be dissolved into something complete and great"?

2. Which satirist's grave reads, "Where fierce indignation can no longer tear his heart"?

3. Which mystery author's gravestone has these lines from Robert Louis Stevenson's poem "My Wife": "STEEL TRUE, BLADE STRAIGHT"?

4. Whose grave is marked with these lines from his own poem: "Cast a cold Eye / On life, on Death. / Horseman, pass by"?

5. "AGAINST YOU I WILL FLING MYSELF, UNVANQUISHED AND UNYIELDING, O DEATH!" is which writer's epitaph?

ANSWERS

1. Willa Cather. The lines are from *My Ántonia*.

2. Jonathan Swift.

3. Arthur Conan Doyle.

4. William Butler Yeats. The lines are the last in "Under Ben Bulben." Additional trivia: Larry McMurtry titled his first novel *Horseman, Pass By*.

5. Virginia Woolf.

DON'T KNOW MUCH ABOUT

James Baldwin

James Baldwin (1924–1987) learned the power of words early in his life: by the age of fourteen he was preaching in Harlem's Fireside Pentecostal Church. Three years later, Baldwin left the church and Harlem for Greenwich Village and, eventually, for Europe, where he pursued a career as a writer. His first novel, *Go Tell It on the Mountain* (1953), was a semiautobiographical coming-of-age story about the family tensions and ultimate religious conversion of fourteen-year-old John Grimes. Better regarded than Baldwin's novels were his essays: Baldwin wrote passionately about black identity, white hypocrisy, and civil rights in America, as well as about war, sexuality, and other political and cultural issues. What do you know about Baldwin? Try this "simple" James Baldwin quiz.

TRUE OR FALSE?

1. James Baldwin argued eloquently that so-called Black English was not a real language.

2. At Frederick Douglass Junior High School, Baldwin studied with the Harlem Renaissance poet Countee Cullen.

3. Novels like *Giovanni's Room* (1956) and *Another Country* (1962) were controversial because they dealt with homosexuality and interracial relationships.

4. The first essay in Baldwin's *The Fire Next Time* (1963) was structured as a letter to white America.

5. Baldwin wrote extensively on American political life from France and never returned to the United States after 1948.

ANSWERS

1. False. Just the opposite: Baldwin called Black English "a language that permits the nation its only glimpse of reality."

2. True. Cullen instructed Baldwin in French.

3. True.

4. False. It was a letter to his fourteen-year-old nephew and namesake, written on the centennial of the Emancipation Proclamation.

5. False. He returned to the United States various times, including in the late 1960s to participate in the civil rights movement and in the 1980s as the Five Colleges Professor of Afro-American Studies at the University of Massachusetts, Amherst.

DON'T KNOW MUCH ABOUT
Willa Cather

Emily Brontë had the Yorkshire Moors, Jack London had the Klondike, William Faulkner the American South. But perhaps no writer is so closely associated with a landscape as Willa Cather (1873–1947) is with the Nebraska prairie. She wrote the following about moving to the Plains, which became the setting for her best-known stories and novels: "So the country and I had it out together and by the end of the first autumn the shaggy grass country had gripped me with a passion that I have never been able to shake. It has been the happiness and curse of my life." Are you gripped by books like *O Pioneers!* (1913) and *My Ántonia* (1918)? Then test your Cather knowledge with this quick quiz.

TRUE OR FALSE?

1. Like Ántonia Shimerda of *My Ántonia*, Willa Cather left Eastern Europe as a child and settled with her family in Nebraska.

2. Much of Willa Cather's prairie fiction takes place in Red Cloud, Nebraska.

3. As a teenager, Cather dressed in men's clothes and signed letters "William Cather, MD."

4. Cather won the Pulitzer Prize for *Death Comes for the Archbishop* (1927).

ANSWERS

1. False. Cather was born in Virgina and moved to Nebraska at age ten—just like Jim Burden, the narrator in *My Ántonia*. The character of Ántonia was based on Annie Sadilek, a girl from Bohemia who worked in the home of Cather's neighbors, the Miners.

2. True. Red Cloud is the actual town where Cather spent her adolescent years.

3. True. Although Cather left behind this male persona (and the dream of becoming a doctor), her sexuality has been the subject of much critical speculation.

4. False. She won for *One of Ours*, in 1923.

DON'T KNOW MUCH ABOUT
Jane Austen

The person, be it gentleman or lady, who has not pleasure in a good novel, must be intolerably stupid.

S o says Henry Tilney, the charming young clergy-man in Jane Austen's *Northanger Abbey*, defending a genre that was taken about as seriously in Austen's time as drugstore romances and "beach reads" are today. Novels, to high-minded early nineteenth-century read-ers, were trashy and sentimental, and only filled wom-en's heads with nonsense. Austen (1775–1817) herself came from a family of voracious readers; she said they were "not ashamed" to read novels. Austen's works, in-cluding favorites like *Emma*, *Pride and Prejudice*, and *Sense and Sensibility*, are marked by a focus on young women in situations similar to her own: educated and imaginative daughters of the middling rich. Unlike her heroines, who depended on marriage to secure their social standing, Austen—as well as her only sister,

Cassandra—never married. Test your own sense of Jane Austen with this quiz.

1. Under what name were Austen's novels published during her lifetime?

2. What is the name of Austen's last, never-completed novel?

3. What was the profession of George Austen, Jane's father?

4. Which of Austen's novels became a movie starring Kate Winslet, Emma Thompson, and Hugh Grant?

5. What film transformed *Pride and Prejudice* into a Bollywood-style musical?

6. Who called Austen "the most perfect artist among women"?

ANSWERS

1. None—they were published anonymously, "By a Lady."

2. *Sanditon.* Several contemporary writers have "completed" the novel, and there are versions of these finished books.

3. Rector. The rectory at Steventon, Hampshire, where Jane Austen wrote three of her novels, was destroyed by fire in 1823.

4. *Sense and Sensibility.*

5. *Bride and Prejudice.*

6. Virginia Woolf.

DON'T KNOW MUCH ABOUT
First Novels

S ome novelists hit the jackpot with their first publication: J. K. Rowling and her debut novel, *Harry
Potter and the Philosopher's Stone* (1997), for example. Other first novels that are still widely read today
include William Golding's *Lord of the Flies* (1954),
Toni Morrison's *The Bluest Eye* (1970), and F. Scott
Fitzgerald's *This Side of Paradise* (1920). But how
many of these overlooked or lesser-known first published novels can you pair with their authors?

1. *Crome Yellow* (1921)

2. *Poor Folk* (1846)

3. *Player Piano* (1952)

4. *The Voyage Out* (1915)

5. *Grimus* (1975)

6. *Jonah's Gourd Vine* (1934)

7. *The Town and the City* (1950)

8. *Cup of Gold* (1929)

ANSWERS

1. Aldous Huxley.

2. Fyodor Dostoyevsky.

3. Kurt Vonnegut.

4. Virginia Woolf.

5. Salman Rushdie.

6. Zora Neale Hurston.

7. Jack Kerouac.

8. John Steinbeck.

DON'T KNOW MUCH ABOUT
Working Titles

*T*rimalchio? *Trimalchio in West Egg?* *Gold-Hatted Gatsby? The High-Bouncing Lover?* Under the *Red White and Blue?* F. Scott Fitzgerald considered all these titles before settling (thankfully!) on *The Great Gatsby*. How many of these novels and poems can you identify by their working titles?

1. *The Hours* (**Virginia Woolf**)

2. *Nobody's Fault* (**Charles Dickens**)

3. *A Moment's Ornament* (**Edith Wharton**)

4. *He Do the Police in Different Voices* (**T. S. Eliot**)

5. *Fiesta* (**Ernest Hemingway**)

6. *Dark House* and *A Dark House* (William Faulkner)

7. *Tomorrow Is Another Day* (No hint here!)

8. *First Impressions* (Jane Austen)

ANSWERS

1. *Mrs. Dalloway.* Michael Cunningham used Woolf's working title for his 1998 novel *The Hours*, based on Woolf's life and work.

2. *Little Dorrit.*

3. *The House of Mirth.* The original title came from the Wordsworth poem "She was a Phantom of delight."

4. "The Waste Land." The line is from Charles Dickens's *Our Mutual Friend*: Betty Higden is praising her adopted son, Sloppy, for reading the newspaper so dramatically.

5. *The Sun Also Rises.*

6. *Light in August* and *Absalom, Absalom!*, respectively.

7. *Gone with the Wind*, by Margaret Mitchell. Mitchell submitted a long list of possible titles to her publisher, including *Tote the Weary Land* and *Ba! Ba! Black Sheep.*

8. *Pride and Prejudice.*

DON'T KNOW MUCH ABOUT
Robert Heinlein

Science fiction has made some remarkable predictions—from submarines (Jules Verne) to air-conditioning (H. G. Wells). What was Robert Heinlein's most prescient sci-fi invention? A manned rocket flight to the moon, dreamed up in a juvenile book called *Rocket Ship Galileo* (1947). Best known as the author of the 1961 novel *Stranger in a Strange Land*—which in many ways predicted the sexual liberation of the 1960s—Heinlein (1907–1988) is one of the most influential science-fiction writers of all time. If you're no stranger to Heinlein's writing, take this sci-fi quiz.

1. What word, coined by Heinlein, does the *American Heritage Dictionary* define as "to understand profoundly through intuition or empathy"?

2. Which Heinlein novel, about an interstellar war between mankind and "Bugs," did the director Paul Verhoeven adapt into a blockbuster movie in 1997?

3. Which government agency posthumously awarded Heinlein a Distinguished Public Service Medal?

4. What 1950 film, based loosely on *Rocket Ship Galileo* and with a screenplay by Heinlein, is considered to have initiated the science-fiction movie boom of the 1950s?

5. What science-fiction writing award did Heinlein win four times for his novels?

ANSWERS

1. "Grok." The word comes from Heinlein's *Stranger in a Strange Land* (1961).

2. *Starship Troopers* (1959).

3. NASA.

4. *Destination Moon.* Heinlein served as technical director for this film, which tried to provide a realistic depiction of the first moon landing.

5. The Science Fiction Achievement Award, better known as the "Hugo," for best novel.

DON'T KNOW MUCH ABOUT
Ayn Rand

*Happiness is that state of consciousness which
proceeds from the achievement of one's values.*

Ayn Rand (1905–1982), who wrote this in *The
Virtue of Selfishness* (1964), preached a philosophy of rational self-interest in both her novels and her
nonfiction. Acting morally, she argued, depends on
pursuing individual goals and developing virtues like
honesty, integrity, and pride. According to Rand, selfishness is not a moral failing, but a strength. Her "ob-
jectivist" philosophy has its counterparts in politics, as
libertarianism, and in economics, as free-market capitalism. Rand's most famous novels, *The Fountainhead*
(1943) and *Atlas Shrugged* (1957), continue to be both
provocative and popular. Take this Ayn Rand quiz to
test your objective knowledge of this author—if you
don't know the answers, just shrug.

1. Which Ayn Rand character—and mouthpiece for Rand's philosophy—stated, "I work for nothing but my own profit"?

2. Who is the hero of *The Fountainhead*—an architect who is "as man should be"?

3. Where was Ayn Rand born?

4. What career did Rand initially pursue in the United States?

5. Which of Ayn Rand's disciples became one of the most powerful men in the world of finance?

ANSWERS

1. John Galt, the hero of *Atlas Shrugged.*

2. Howard Roark.

3. Saint Petersburg, Russia. Her family fled to the Crimea (now an autonomous region in Ukraine) soon after the 1917 Bolshevik Revolution. She returned to the city, then called Petrograd, as a student, but later left the Soviet Union for good, arriving in New York in 1926.

4. Screenwriting. She wrote the screenplay adaptation for *The Fountainhead,* a 1949 film starring Gary Cooper.

5. Alan Greenspan, former chairman of the Federal Reserve, who belonged to the group of Rand's friends and followers known as the "Collective."

DON'T KNOW MUCH ABOUT
Edgar Allan Poe

E dgar Allan Poe (1809–1849) wrote some of the darkest, strangest poems and stories in the English language. His narrators, who generally speak in the first person, have led many readers to confuse Poe with his deeply disturbed characters: opium users, sufferers of paranoia and delusions, sinister murderers. Aspects of the author's strange life and death add to that confusion. In October 1849, Dr. J. E. Snodgrass, a friend of Poe's, was summoned to a Baltimore tavern where he found Poe half-conscious and dressed in someone else's clothes. Speculation on the cause of his death has ranged from delirium tremens, to injuries sustained during a beating, to rabies. Think you know Poe? Take this quiz, and you shouldn't need to "ponder weak and weary."

1. How old was Edgar Allan Poe's cousin, Virginia Clemm, when the author married her in 1836?

2. In which of Poe's stories does the narrator hear "a low, dull, quick sound—much such a sound as a watch makes when enveloped in cotton"?

3. In which story does Montresor kill Fortunado by immurement—walling him in and leaving him to die?

4. What is the name of Poe's brilliant and extremely rational detective, who appears in "The Purloined Letter," "The Murders in the Rue Morgue," and "The Mystery of Marie Rogêt"?

5. The first Halloween special of the television cartoon series *The Simpsons* featured a segment based on Poe's famous poem "The Raven." Instead of "Nevermore," what phrase did the raven (a Bart Simpson look-alike) repeat incessantly?

ANSWERS

1. Thirteen. He was twenty-seven. After her death eleven years later, he addressed the poem "Annabel Lee" to her.

2. "The Tell-Tale Heart."

3. "The Cask of Amontillado."

4. C. Auguste Dupin.

5. "Eat my shorts." Although Poe died in 1849, he was credited as a writer for this 1990 television show.

DON'T KNOW MUCH ABOUT
E. M. Forster

Yes—oh, dear, yes—the novel tells a story.

This was E. M. Forster's famously simple answer to his own question, "What does a novel do?" Sounds easy enough, but the stories he told in his novels were good enough to keep readers—and filmgoers—enthralled for years. Forster (1879–1970) wrote *Where Angels Fear to Tread* (1905), *A Room with a View* (1908), *Howards End* (1910), and *A Passage to India* (1924)—all of which are now popular movies as well as books. In his novels, Forster showed British characters, at home and abroad, learning to let passion into their otherwise practical lives. Make a passage into the world of Forster with this quick quiz.

1. **Which two E. M. Forster novels are set in Italy?**

2. Which book, Forster's only novel to deal with homosexuality, was not published until after his death?

3. What opera, based on a story by Herman Melville, features a libretto cowritten by E. M. Forster?

4. Who is the heroine of *A Room with a View*?

ANSWERS

1. *A Room with a View* and *Where Angels Fear to Tread.*

2. *Maurice* (1971). That Forster was gay was not widely publicized during his lifetime.

3. *Billy Budd, Sailor,* by Benjamin Britten. Eric Crozier cowrote the libretto with Forster.

4. Lucy Honeychurch.

DON'T KNOW MUCH ABOUT
Don Quixote

M ost of us know the story of Miguel de Cervantes's *Don Quixote*—whether we've seen it as a ballet, heard it as a musical, or watched it as a Mr. Magoo cartoon. Alonso Quixano, a gentleman in the Spanish countryside, renames himself "Don Quixote de la Mancha" and embarks on a series of ridiculous misadventures as a knight. Dressed in an old suit of armor and riding a bony horse, Don Quixote sets out to win the love of "Dulcinea del Taboso"—actually a local farm girl. *Don Quixote*, published in 1605 and 1615, poked fun at novels exaggerating the heroics of knights; it also highlighted an idealist's frustrations in a materialistic world. You don't need to dream the impossible dream to learn more about *Don Quixote*—just take this quick quiz.

1. What does Don Quixote mistakenly attack, thinking that it is a giant?

2. Who is Don Quixote's sidekick?

3. What is the source of Don Quixote's illusions?

4. Who, in *Don Quixote*, is Cide Hamete Benengeli?

5. Who are Rocinante and Dapple?

ANSWERS

1. A windmill. This is where the phrase "to tilt at windmills," meaning to fight an imaginary enemy, came from. The scene also inspired a 1971 movie called *They Might Be Giants*, from which the popular band took its name.

2. Sancho Panza, a peasant whom Don Quixote makes his squire.

3. He has read too many chivalric romances, or books about the adventures of knights.

4. The fictional author of the tale. Cervantes writes that he has translated the work of this Moorish writer into Spanish.

5. Don Quixote's horse and Sancho Panza's mule.

DON'T KNOW MUCH ABOUT
Homer's Odyssey

Very little is known about Homer, the Greek poet credited with writing the eighth century BCE masterpiece the *Odyssey*—in fact, some scholars wonder if the "blind bard" ever existed at all. One thing is clear: the *Odyssey* itself is remarkable. Not only does it tell the exciting story of Odysseus's adventures with witches, gods, and monsters, but it also pioneered the use of storytelling techniques like the flashback to create suspense. This has led many to dub the *Odyssey* the first novel—even though it's a poem. Know whether Odysseus makes it home to Ithaca? Take this quick quiz about the classic epic.

1. **Which epic poem is the prequel to the** *Odyssey*?

2. What kind of creature is Polyphemus?

3. What do three of Odysseus's soldiers eat, causing them to forget everything?

4. At the beginning of the *Odyssey*, who offers Odysseus immortality if he remains with her as her lover?

5. What spell does the witch Circe work on Odysseus's men?

6. Where must Odysseus travel to meet with the prophet Tiresias?

ANSWERS

1. The *Iliad*. Though some scholars question whether one person wrote both poems, there is a general consensus that the *Iliad* and the *Odyssey* are the work of a single author.

2. A Cyclops—one of a race of one-eyed giants.

3. Lotus, in the Land of the Lotus-Eaters.

4. Calypso. A nymph, she is the daughter of Atlas and keeps Odysseus captive on the island of Ogygia for seven years.

5. She turns them into pigs.

6. Hades, the underworld of Greek mythology.

DON'T KNOW MUCH ABOUT
Oscar Wilde

We are all in the gutter, but some of us are
looking at the stars.

O scar Wilde noted that in his play, *Lady Wind-ermere's Fan* (1892). Wilde (1854–1900) believed in aestheticism—"art for art's sake"—and wrote in order to please, charm, and delight readers and audiences. Though the novel *The Picture of Dorian Gray* (1891) and plays like *The Importance of Being Earnest* (1895) were critical successes, Wilde drew more attention for the sensational 1895 trial in which he was accused, and found guilty, of "gross indecency"—a nineteenth-century euphemism for homosexuality. He was sentenced to two years of hard labor, a prison term that left Wilde physically and emotionally devastated, and he died a few years after his release. What do you know about this stargazing author? Take this quiz and see.

206 · KENNETH C. DAVIS & JENNY DAVIS

1. Where does the phrase "the love that dare not speak its name" come from?

2. Which of Wilde's plays did Richard Strauss adapt as an opera?

3. Why did Wilde publish his poem "The Ballad of Reading Gaol" under the name "C.3.3"?

4. Who was Sebastian Melmoth?

ANSWERS

1. The poem "Two Loves," by Lord Alfred Douglas, who was Wilde's close friend and lover. During questioning by the prosecution in his trial, Wilde clarified the meaning of the phrase as "a great affection of an elder for a younger man."*

2. *Salomé* (1892; *Salome*, the English version, 1894). Strauss's opera debuted in 1905 and earned infamy for its racy "dance of the seven veils."

3. It was his cell number in prison.

4. Oscar Wilde himself: after his imprisonment, Wilde lived under the name Sebastian Melmoth. That surname came from *Melmoth the Wanderer* (1820), a gothic novel by Wilde's great-uncle Charles Maturin.

---

* http://www.phrases.org.uk/meanings/364900.html

DON'T KNOW MUCH ABOUT
Pablo Neruda

Poetry is like bread; it should be shared by all,
by scholars and by peasants, by all our vast,
incredible, extraordinary family of humanity.

So wrote Pablo Neruda. Millions have shared and enjoyed the poetry of Neruda (1904–1973), whose body of work includes sensual love sonnets, lyrical epics, political poems, and odes to the commonest objects: a lemon, a book, a pair of socks. Those odes, which are among his best-loved works, reflect what Neruda said in his 1971 Nobel Prize lecture: "the best poet is he who prepares our daily bread: the nearest baker who does not imagine himself to be a god."* Have a slice or two of Neruda, then take this quick quiz.

---

* http://nobelprize.org/nobel_prizes/literature/laureates/1971/neruda-lecture-e.html

1. What country was Neruda from?

2. In which book did Neruda chronicle five hundred years of Latin American history?

3. What everyday object did Neruda hail as a "constant constellation, / round rose of water"?

4. Which poet's framed portrait did Neruda keep in his home?

5. In what popular film is Neruda a central character?

ANSWERS

1. Chile.

2. *Canto General* (1943). Of more than three hundred poems in the collection, the best known is "The Heights of Machu Picchu."

3. An onion, in "Ode to the Onion."

4. Walt Whitman. When a carpenter hanging Whitman's portrait asked Neruda if the picture was of his grandfather, Neruda answered yes.*

5. Michael Radford's *Il Postino* (*The Postman, 1994*).

---

* http://www.english.emory.edu/Bahri/Neruda.html

DON'T KNOW MUCH ABOUT
First Lines from Drama

Stage lights come up on a two-story building on a New Orleans street. The music of a "blue piano" can be heard. Then the audience, listening intently, hears the iconic first words of Tennessee Williams's *A Streetcar Named Desire*: "Hey, there! Stella, Baby!" Think you know how other great playwrights have broken the silence? Take a brief intermission to identify these opening lines from favorite plays.

1. One out, a man on, bottom of the seventh, two balls, no strikes.

2. How beautiful is the princess Salome tonight?

3. Ismene, dear sister, you would think that we had already suffered enough for the curse on Oedipus.

4. Hide the Christmas tree away carefully, Helene. The children mustn't see it till this evening when it's decorated.

5. Yes, I have tricks in my pocket. I have things up my sleeve.

6. Nothing to be done.

7. Would that the *Argo* had never winged its way to the land of Colchis through the dark-blue Symplegades!

8. She'll live.

ANSWERS

1. Neil Simon, *Brighton Beach Memoirs* (1982).

2. Oscar Wilde, *Salome* (1894).

3. Sophocles, *Antigone* (c. 441 BCE).

4. Henrik Ibsen, *A Doll's House* (1879).

5. Tennessee Williams, *The Glass Menagerie* (1945).

6. Samuel Beckett, *Waiting for Godot* (1953).

7. Euripides, *Medea* (431 BCE).

8. William Gibson, *The Miracle Worker* (1961).

DON'T KNOW MUCH ABOUT
Dante's Divine Comedy

Abandon all hope, ye who enter here.

These chilling words are inscribed across the gates of hell in Dante's *Inferno*. In that book-length poem, the Italian poet Dante Alighieri (1265–1321) chronicled his own imaginary journey through the underworld. The next two books, *Purgatorio* and *Paradiso*, follow Dante through purgatory and into heaven, where he could be reunited with his true love. The trilogy is referred to as *The Divine Comedy*—although its author called it simply the *Commedia* (or "Comedy")—and was revolutionary because Dante wrote it in the spoken Italian dialect of Tuscany, rather than in Latin, the literary language. What do you know about Dante and his divine trilogy? Don't abandon all hope—just take this quick quiz!

1. In the first two books of *The Divine Comedy*, who is Dante's guide?

2. What is the name of the woman whom Dante loves?

3. Did Dante, writing in the early fourteenth century, believe the world was flat?

4. Which artist, known for his surrealist work, created a complete set of illustrations for the three books of *The Divine Comedy*?

5. Is there a lake of fire in the center of Dante's hell?

ANSWERS

1. Virgil, the Roman poet who wrote the *Aeneid*. Virgil leads Dante through hell and purgatory, but they eventually part because, as a pagan, Virgil cannot enter Christian heaven.

2. Beatrice. Though in real life Dante hardly knew Beatrice Portinari (and was married to someone else), his idealized love for her inspired much of his writing—including *The Divine Comedy*, in which she appears as his true love and his guide to heaven.

3. No. Dante (the character) journeys to the center of a globe-shaped earth to get to the deepest reaches of hell, and he climbs up and out to purgatory.

4. Salvador Dalí. Dante's work has also inspired illustrations by Sandro Botticelli, Gustave Doré, and William Blake, among many others.

5. No. There is a lake of ice.

DON'T KNOW MUCH ABOUT
Leo Tolstoy

Henry James called it a "loose baggy monster." Others called it a masterpiece. And Woody Allen joked that he'd taken a speed-reading course and read it in twenty minutes: "It's about Russia." *War and Peace*, probably the most famous and certainly the longest novel by Leo Tolstoy (1828–1910), is a hefty read, but it rewards readers with a panorama of romance, drama, and history. How much detail did Tolstoy put into *War and Peace*? The novel focuses on the lives of several major characters, like the lovable Natasha Rostova, but includes more than five hundred characters! What do you know about this epic book and the monumental author who wrote it? Take this Tolstoy quiz and test your knowledge.

218 · KENNETH C. DAVIS & JENNY DAVIS

1. Which novel was Tolstoy reputedly inspired to write after he viewed the body of a woman who had thrown herself under a train?

2. Which Tolstoy book began as a historical novel about an exiled Decembrist (a rebel in the 1825 revolt against the Russian czar)?

3. In which treatise did Tolstoy argue that art should be morally uplifting?

4. Which of Tolstoy's title characters is forced into a spiritual crisis by illness?

5. Which spots do Tolstoy's books fill on *Time* magazine's top-ten list of novels?

ANSWERS

1. *Anna Karenina.*

2. *War and Peace.* Tolstoy eventually chose to set the novel earlier, around the time of Napoleon's 1812 invasion of Russia.

3. *What Is Art?* (1897–1898).

4. Ivan Ilyich, in *The Death of Ivan Ilyich.* This 1886 story reflected Tolstoy's own crisis of faith, which he describes in *A Confession* (1879–1881).

5. *Anna Karenina* at #1 and *War and Peace* at #3.

DON'T KNOW MUCH ABOUT
Paradise Lost

Of man's first disobedience, and the fruit
Of that forbidden tree, whose mortal taste
Brought death into the world, and all our woe.

This is the story told in *Paradise Lost*, the twelve-book poem by John Milton (1608–1674). In this Bible-inspired epic, Satan learns of the world that God has created and sets out to corrupt Adam and Eve. What ensues is a battle between good and evil, fought on a cosmic stage that encompasses heaven, hell, chaos, and the fledgling earth. If you've ever gotten lost in Milton's epic work, take this quick quiz to test your knowledge.

TRUE OR FALSE?

1. Milton was blind when he wrote *Paradise Lost*.

2. Because he wanted to create a British national epic, Milton considered writing a long poem about his hero, Henry VIII.

3. Milton's sequel to *Paradise Lost* was called *Paradise Found*, and it told the biblical story of Moses's exodus from Egypt.

4. The city in hell where Satan and his fallen angels dwell is called "Dis."

5. Before Adam and Eve's fall and expulsion from Eden, Satan comes to paradise in the form of a mist.

6. The line "better to reign in hell than serve in heaven" inspired a famous *Star Trek* episode and film.

ANSWERS

1. True. Each day, he dictated lines of verse to his daughters, who wrote them down for him.

2. False. Milton did consider writing an epic about the life of his political hero: Oliver Cromwell, the Puritan leader of the short-lived Commonwealth of England. He also considered a poem about King Arthur and the knights of the Round Table.

3. False. The sequel, *Paradise Regained* (1671), told the story of Jesus's temptation by Satan.

4. False. Satan and his fellow devils live in "Pandemonium"—a word created by Milton that means "all the demons." Dis is the city in the sixth circle of hell in Dante's *Inferno.*

5. True. He then transforms into a serpent and tempts Eve to eat the forbidden fruit.

6. True. The line is spoken by Khan, the villain featured in "Space Seed" and the feature film *The Wrath of Khan.*

DON'T KNOW MUCH ABOUT
Albert Camus

I feel more fellowship with the defeated
than with saints.

So says Dr. Bernard Rieux in Albert Camus's 1947 novel *The Plague*. Rieux continues: "Heroism and sanctity don't really appeal to me, I imagine. What interests me is being a man." With characters like Rieux—a doctor doing his best to treat victims of a mysterious plague—Albert Camus (1913–1960) explored mankind's noble but hopeless struggle against suffering and death. His novels, including *The Plague* and *The Stranger* (1942), explore his philosophy of the "absurd": the impossible task of finding meaning in human existence. If you're no stranger to Camus, take this quick quiz to test your knowledge.

TRUE OR FALSE?

1. Camus grew up in the French colony of Martinique.

2. As a student, Camus was an excellent soccer player and dreamed of playing professionally.

3. Camus based his famous essay about absurdity on the Greek myth of Icarus, who drowned after flying too close to the sun with wings made of wax.

4. Because he believed that life was inherently meaningless, Camus was politically apathetic and practiced disengagement from political affairs.

5. Camus believed in suicide and took his own life.

6. Camus was the second-youngest winner of the Noble Prize in Literature.

ANSWERS

1. False. Camus was born and raised in Algeria, where many of his stories and novels are set. The term for French nationals in Algeria was *pied-noir*, meaning "black foot."

2. True. He played goalie but gave up this dream when he contracted tuberculosis.

3. False. Camus wrote about Sisyphus, who was condemned by the gods to push a boulder up a mountain, only to see it roll down again, for eternity. The essay, which likened human life to Sisyphus's punishment, was called "The Myth of Sisyphus" (1942).

4. False. During World War II, Camus was a member of the French Resistance and published the underground newspaper *Combat*. He did not, however, support Algerian independence.

5. False. He died in a car accident and did not advocate suicide.

6. True. When he won in 1957, he was second youngest after Rudyard Kipling. Camus was the first winner born in Africa.

DON'T KNOW MUCH ABOUT
Frankenstein

"It's alive... It's alive!" Although Victor Frankenstein never actually cries out these words in the 1818 novel by Mary Shelley (1797–1851), her story and its characters have taken on a life of their own. Frankenstein, a student, morphed into the prototypical mad scientist, while the monster that he brought to life became a stock character for generations of horror films. Bring your Frankenstein knowledge to life with this quick quiz.

1. **What is the full title of Shelley's *Frankenstein*?**

2. **What is the monster's name in Shelley's novel?**

3. What actor starred in the classic horror flicks *Frankenstein* (1931), *Bride of Frankenstein* (1935), and *Son of Frankenstein* (1939)?

4. In Shelley's book, does Victor Frankenstein create a bride for his monster?

5. What actor and director, known for his film adaptations of Shakespeare, attempted a film version of *Frankenstein* that tried to be loyal to Shelley's work?

6. Shelley begins her novel with a quotation: "Did I request thee, Maker, from my clay / To mould me Man? Did I solicit thee / From darkness to promote me?" From what epic poem did she take these lines?

ANSWERS

1. *Frankenstein; or, The Modern Prometheus.* Prometheus was the character in Greek mythology who stole fire from the gods.

2. He does not have one. Although he is popularly called "Frankenstein," this has no basis in Shelley's book.

3. Boris Karloff.

4. He does, but he destroys her before bringing her to life.

5. Kenneth Branagh. He directed and starred in *Mary Shelley's Frankenstein* (1994).

6. *Paradise Lost,* by John Milton. They are Adam's words, after the fall.

DON'T KNOW MUCH ABOUT
Gustave Flaubert

Tolstoy's Anna Karenina. Hawthorne's Hester Prynne. Adulteresses are at the center of some of the best-loved nineteenth-century novels, and no list of them would be complete without Flaubert's Emma Bovary. Gustave Flaubert (1821–1880) created a sympathetic and very human heroine for his most famous work, *Madame Bovary* (1856–1857): Emma is a farmer's daughter stifled by her rural life and dull marriage, and is drawn into moral and financial ruin. Flaubert himself sympathized with Emma Bovary so much, in fact, that he once declared, "Madame Bovary, c'est moi." Have you had a "sentimental education" in Flaubert's fiction? If so, test your knowledge with this quick quiz.

1. What is the name of Emma Bovary's husband, a kind but simple country doctor?

2. What escapist pastime does Emma Bovary share with Anna Karenina?

3. Which of Flaubert's novels features a young man and his romantic pursuit of an older, married woman?

4. For which novel were Flaubert and his publishers put on trial for immorality?

5. In *Time* magazine's 2007 list of greatest novels, where does *Madame Bovary* rank?

ANSWERS

1. Charles Bovary.

2. Reading. Both heroines search for the kind of romance they've read about—Flaubert writes in *Madame Bovary,* for example, "Emma tried to find out what one meant exactly in life by the words felicity, passion, rapture, that had seemed to her so beautiful in books."

3. *A Sentimental Education* (1869).

4. *Madame Bovary.* Flaubert was acquitted after his lawyers convinced the jury that the novel in fact cautioned against immorality.

5. At #2, behind *Anna Karenina.*

DON'T KNOW MUCH ABOUT
Jack London

In the early twentieth century, American readers went wild for a pair of books by Jack London (1876–1916). First, *The Call of the Wild* (1903) told the story of Buck, a dog who returns to the ways of his wolf ancestors. Then London published the mirror image of that tale with *White Fang* (1906), about the journey of a half-wolf, half-dog to a loving human family. If you've heard the call of Jack London, sink your teeth into this quiz.

TRUE OR FALSE?

1. London based Buck, the canine hero of *The Call of the Wild*, on a dog named "Jack" that he had met in the Klondike.

2. *The epigraph that London uses to begin* The Call of the Wild *is a fragment of the Yukon writer Robert Service's poem, "The Call of the Wild."*

3. While serving time in jail for vagrancy, London developed a personal philosophy that combined individualism and socialism.

4. After making a small fortune as a gold prospector, London spent the last twenty years of his life writing in Alaska.

5. London's "To Build a Fire" was a popular how-to book about wilderness survival.

ANSWERS

1. True. Other characters were based on dogs that London had read about in the Reverend Egerton Young's *My Dogs in the Northland*.

2. False. These four lines—"Old longings nomadic leap, / Chafing at custom's chain; / Again from its brumal sleep / Wakens the ferine strain"— come from John M. O'Hara's poem "Atavism." As a biological term, "atavism" refers to the reappearance of an ancestral trait that had disappeared from a line of organisms.

3. True. In 1894, London spent a month mulling over the writings of Marx and Nietzsche in New York's Erie County Penitentiary. He was arrested after he abandoned a protest march of unemployed men, called "Coxey's Army."

4. False. London went north in search of gold in the Klondike (in the Yukon Territory) in 1897, but he stayed for only one year. Like most, he never struck it rich.

5. False. "To Build a Fire" (1908) is one of London's most famous short stories, about a man and a dog traveling on the Yukon Trail in extreme cold.

DON'T KNOW MUCH ABOUT
Robert Louis Stevenson

Chances are, most of what you know about pirates came from *Treasure Island* (1883). From Long John Silver's peg leg and talking parrot, to the legend of the "black spot," to "Yo-ho-ho, and a bottle of rum!" Robert Louis Stevenson (1850–1894) introduced it all to readers in his popular pirate yarn. He followed *Treasure Island* with many more books, including *The Strange Case of Dr. Jekyll and Mr. Hyde* (1886), a chilling psychological tale, and *Kidnapped* (also 1886), a historical novel. If you're feeling adventurous, take this quick Stevenson quiz.

1. **In *Treasure Island*, what phrase does Cap'n Flint (Long John Silver's parrot) repeat endlessly?**

2. Which movie replaces Long John Silver's parrot with a lobster named Polly, and Ben Gunn with "Benjamina"?

3. What does the term "black spot" mean?

4. What is Mr. Hyde's first name?

5. What book was Stevenson's sequel to *Kidnapped*?

ANSWERS

1. "Pieces of eight!" Pieces of eight were silver coins worth eight Spanish *reales*.

2. *Muppet Treasure Island* (1996). Benjamina Gunn is played by Miss Piggy.

3. It is a pirate's death sentence. The "black spot" itself is a piece of paper with a black circle that is handed to a condemned pirate.

4. Edward. Dr. Jekyll's name is Henry.

5. *Catriona* (1893).

DON'T KNOW MUCH ABOUT
Ursula K. Le Guin

Before there was Harry Potter, there was Ged. In the 1968 fantasy novel *A Wizard of Earthsea*, Ursula K. Le Guin's hero emerged as a boy, gifted but sometimes reckless, learning wizardry and struggling with powerful forces of darkness. Le Guin (b. 1929) followed Ged and a young priestess named Tenar through a series of books set in Earthsea, including *The Tombs of Atuan* (1970) and *The Farthest Shore* (1972). More than just a fantasy or young-adult writer, Le Guin has proved her versatility over the last half century with works of science fiction as well as with realistic novels, screenplays, critical essays, and translations. Think you're a wizard of all things Le Guin? Take this quick quiz and see how you fare.

1. In the Earthsea novels, what is Ged's commonly used name?

2. What Chinese-language classic did Le Guin spend forty years translating?

3. Which classic epic poem provided inspiration—and the title character—for Le Guin's 2008 novel *Lavinia*?

4. Which Le Guin sci-fi novel features George Orr, a character whose dreams influence reality?

5. Which Earthsea sequel did not come out until 1990—eighteen years after the last book in the Earthsea trilogy?

ANSWERS

1. Sparrowhawk. Ged is his "true name"—a name too powerful to be spoken casually. More name trivia: before becoming a wizard, he was called "Duny."

2. The *Tao Te Ching*, by Lao Tzu. Taoist elements, like the continuous interplay of darkness and light, can be found in many of Le Guin's books.

3. The *Aeneid*, by Virgil. Lavinia is the woman who, at the end of the epic, will marry Aeneas; in Virgil's poem, however, she never speaks.

4. *The Lathe of Heaven* (1971). In the novel, a therapist tries to harness the power of Orr's dreams in order to create a utopia.

5. *Tehanu: The Last Book of Earthsea.*

DON'T KNOW MUCH ABOUT
Stephen King

All work and no play makes Jack a dull boy. Luckily for readers, though, Stephen King has kept his writing thrilling and imaginative despite a reputation as one of the hardest-working writers in the business. King (b. 1947) has written dozens of bestselling novels, many of which have become classic horror movies: *Carrie* (1974), *Salem's Lot* (1974), *The Shining* (1977), *The Stand* (1978), *Firestarter* (1980), *Cujo* (1981), *It* (1986), and *Misery* (1987), just to name a handful. King is so prolific that, for years, he published books both under his own name and also under a pen name to avoid flooding the market with more than one "Stephen King" thriller a year. What do you know about the King of Horror? Take this quiz to test your knowledge.

1. What was King's first published novel?

2. What was Stephen King's pen name for novels like *Running Man* (1983) and *The Long Walk* (1979)?

3. What was King's first published work of non-fiction?

4. What Stephen King novella—a departure from the horror genre—was set in a Maine penitentiary?

5. Who directed the 1980 film version of *The Shining*?

6. King's baseball fanaticism is well known. What team does he root for?

ANSWERS

1. *Carrie* (1974).

2. Richard Bachman. King says that he got the last name from the band Bachman Turner Overdrive.

3. *Danse Macabre* (1980). In the book, King reflected on the horror genre and on influences on his own work.

4. *Rita Hayworth and the Shawshank Redemption* (1982). The 1994 movie *The Shawshank Redemption* was based on this book.

5. Stanley Kubrick.

6. The Boston Red Sox.

DON'T KNOW MUCH ABOUT
Obscene Books

In defining "obscenity," Associate Justice Potter Stewart wrote in a 1964 Supreme Court decision, "I know it when I see it." People have been arguing over obscenity and pornography—which in the original Greek means "to write about prostitutes"—almost since there was writing. For publishers the label has been a mixed blessing. Books have been burned, banned from the mails, and yanked from library shelves. But the phrase "Banned in Boston" eventually became a favorite selling slogan. And many books once deemed "dirty" are now bona fide classics. Know obscenity when you see it? Unwrap the plain brown paper around this quiz about some notorious "obscene" books.

1. Which hefty novel depicts a character reading *Titbits* magazine on the toilet, allowing "his bowels to ease themselves quietly as he read"?

2. Which D. H. Lawrence novel was banned in the United Kingdom and not published there until three decades after the author's death?

3. Which autobiographical novel did poet Ezra Pound once call "a dirty book worth reading"?

4. Which 1881 poetry collection, now considered an American classic, was withdrawn from circulation by its publisher under a district attorney's threat of obscenity charges?

ANSWERS

1. *Ulysses* (1922), by James Joyce. The character described is Leopold Bloom.

2. *Lady Chatterley's Lover* (1928). The first UK printing was in 1960, after a trial in which literary lights like E. M. Forster took the stand to defend the novel. In the end the prosecution was simply behind the times: counsel Mervyn Griffith-Jones at one point asked the jurors, "Is it a book you would wish your wife or servants to read?"

3. *Tropic of Cancer*, by Henry Miller. The novel was published in France in 1934 but was banned in the United States until 1961.

4. Walt Whitman's *Leaves of Grass* (1881 edition).*
In 1865, Whitman had been dismissed from his day job as a clerk in the Bureau of Indian Affairs after James Harlan, secretary of the interior, found and read a working copy of *Leaves of Grass* and considered it obscene.**

---

* http://www.whitmanarchive.org/criticism/current/encyclopedia/entry_26.html

** http://www.whitmanarchive.org/criticism/current/encyclopedia/entry_78.html

DON'T KNOW MUCH ABOUT
Banned Books

Congress Shall Make No Law Respecting an
Establishment of Religion, or Prohibiting the
Free Exercise Thereof; or Abridging the Freedom
of Speech, or of the Press; or the Right of the
People Peaceably to Assemble, and To Petition the
Government for a Redress of Grievances.

That is your First Amendment. It seems pretty self-explanatory. But it causes considerable controversy. Chief among those controversies is the quest to control speech and other forms of expression—like books. The American Library Association does a vigorous job of monitoring attempts to remove books from public schools and libraries. In 2006 the ALA released a list entitled "Most Challenged Books of the Twenty-first Century (2000–2005)." Identify these top five "dangerous" books and their authors by their literary crimes.

1. Promoting witchcraft. (That's all the hint you get.)

2. Vulgar language and violence, in a 1974 novel about bullying and nonconformity.

3. Depictions of sexuality in a series about a high school girl.

4. Profanity and its "portrayal of Jesus" in an American Depression-era classic.

5. References to lebianism, premarital sex, cohabitation, pornography, and violence, in a 1969 autobiography.

ANSWERS

1. The Harry Potter series, by J. K. Rowling

2. *The Chocolate War*, by Robert Cormier.

3. The Alice series, by Phyllis Reynolds Naylor.

4. *Of Mice and Men*, by John Steinbeck.

5. *I Know Why the Caged Bird Sings*, by the poet Maya Angelou, who spoke at Bill Clinton's 1993 inauguration, the first poet to do so since Robert Frost in 1961.

DON'T KNOW MUCH ABOUT

Leslie Marmon Silko

You should understand the way it was back then,
because it is the same even now.

So wrote Leslie Marmon Silko in *Storyteller* (1981). Silko (b. 1948) draws on the past—on traditional Laguna Pueblo stories and on her Pueblo, white, and Mexican heritage—to create poems and stories that are relevant to current times. Her first novel, *Ceremony* (1977), intertwines tribal mythology with the story of a veteran returning to the Laguna Pueblo reservation. Silko is considered one of the foremost writers of the so-called Native American Renaissance, an explosion of works by such Native American authors as the Kiowa writer N. Scott Momaday and the Ojibwe writer Louise Erdrich. Test what you know about this modern-day storyteller with a quick Silko quiz.

1. **What collection of poems was Silko's first published book?**

2. From what war had Tayo, the main character in *Ceremony*, returned?

3. Which character from Laguna Pueblo mythology appears often in Silko's fiction, as well as in the title of her essay collection on contemporary Native American life?

4. *The Delicacy and Strength of Lace* (1986) was a collection of letters between Silko and which Pulitzer Prize–winning American poet?

5. In what epic novel does Silko describe the time since the Americas were colonized as the "epoch of Death-Eye dog"?

ANSWERS

1. *Laguna Woman* (1974).

2. World War II, although the book was written at a time when many soldiers had returned from fighting in Vietnam.

3. Yellow Woman, who in traditional stories saved the Pueblo people from starvation. The essay collection is *Yellow Woman and a Beauty of the Spirit* (1997).

4. James Wright.

5. *Almanac of the Dead* (1991).

DON'T KNOW MUCH ABOUT
Arthur Miller

> *Nothing's planted. I don't have a seed*
> *in the ground.*

With that line, the playwright Arthur Miller (1915–2005) exposed the emptiness of the American Dream through the voice of Willy Loman, the lead character in *Death of a Salesman* (1949). The traveling man who insisted that "a salesman is got to dream," Loman stood for a generation of Americans whose sense of worth was measured only in material success. Think you know Arthur Miller and his plays? If so, this little quiz shouldn't be a hard sell.

1. **Which Hollywood starlet married Arthur Miller in 1956?**

2. **Which Arthur Miller play, set in colonial times, attacked the anti–Communist hysteria of the McCarthy era?**

3. Which director, well known for his work in Hollywood, won Tony awards for his productions of *All My Sons* (1947) and *Death of a Salesman* (1949)?

4. Miller's *An Enemy of the People* (1950) was an adaptation of an 1881 play by which Norwegian dramatist?

5. Who did Miller say were "people who can't sing or dance"?

6. Which Miller play was inspired by a notable failed marriage?

ANSWERS

1. Marilyn Monroe. The couple divorced in 1961, a year and a half before Monroe's death.

2. *The Crucible* (1953), a drama about the Salem witch trials. Several years after the debut of *The Crucible*, Arthur Miller was called to testify before the House of Representatives' Un-American Activities Committee, or HUAC, where he refused to identify other writers as Communists.

3. Elia Kazan, who went on to direct films like *A Streetcar Named Desire* (1951), *On the Waterfront* (1954), and *East of Eden* (1955). Kazan and Miller were close friends, but they became estranged after Kazan identified eight of his colleagues as Communists in his 1952 HUAC testimony.

4. Henrik Ibsen.

5. Critics.

6. *After the Fall*, a thinly veiled portrait of his marriage to Marilyn Monroe.

DON'T KNOW MUCH ABOUT
C. S. Lewis

Imagine stepping out of your everyday world and into a snowy, magical kingdom. Well, C. S. Lewis's *The Lion, the Witch, and the Wardrobe* (1950) allowed readers young and old to do just that. C. S. Lewis (1898–1963) taught medieval literature at Oxford University and later at Cambridge, and he incorporated his love of folklore and his Christian principles into the crowd-pleasing fantasies of the Chronicles of Narnia series. Now, shut the wardrobe doors and step into a quiz about C. S. Lewis.

TRUE OR FALSE?

1. Lewis was born in Belfast, Northern Ireland.

2. The Chronicles of Narnia is a trilogy of fantasy books.

3. C. S. Lewis vehemently denied that rival author J. R. R. Tolkien had influenced his books in any way.

4. Although known for his defense of religion in classics like *The Screwtape Letters* (1942), Lewis was for many years an atheist.

5. Before the Narnia books, Lewis published a trilogy of science fiction novels about interplanetary travel.

ANSWERS

1. True. He was sent to school in England in 1908, just after his mother's death.

2. False. There are seven books in the Narnia series (making it a "heptalogy"), beginning with *The Lion, the Witch, and the Wardrobe* and ending with *The Last Battle* (1956).

3. False. The authors, both of whom taught at Oxford, were close friends. In the 1930s and 1940s, Lewis and Tolkien belonged to a group of intellectuals called the Inklings, and met weekly to discuss their works in progress.

4. True. Lewis, raised Protestant, made a gradual journey from nonbeliever to Anglican. His final conversion to Christianity was sparked by a late-night discussion with two friends, one of whom was J. R. R. Tolkien, a Roman Catholic.

5. True. Moral allegories referred to as the "Cosmic Trilogy," these books are *Out of the Silent Planet* (1938), *Perelandra* (1943), and *That Hideous Strength* (1945). They are set on Mars, Venus, and Earth, respectively.

DON'T KNOW MUCH ABOUT
H. G. Wells

"Time traveler." "Time machine." These phrases, now familiar staples of science fiction, wowed readers when they first appeared in H. G. Wells's *The Time Machine: An Invention* (1895). In that and other remarkably creative novels, Wells (1866–1946) combined his training as a biologist with his concerns for the fate of humankind. The results have become classics of early science fiction: books like *The Island of Dr. Moreau* (1896), *The Invisible Man: A Grotesque Romance* (1897), and *The War of the Worlds* (1898). Now if you've got the time, test yourself with this quick H. G. Wells quiz.

1. **What were the two races descended from humans called in *The Time Machine*?**

2. In *The Island of Dr. Moreau*, what controversial research method had caused Dr. Moreau to be "howled out of" England?

3. From what planet are the invaders in *The War of the Worlds*?

4. Why is Orson Welles's 1938 radio performance of *War of the Worlds* considered the most famous radio broadcast of all time?

5. As a biology student, Wells studied under Thomas Henry Huxley, the grandfather of Aldous Huxley and an outspoken proponent of which famous scientist's theories?

ANSWERS

1. The Morlocks and the Eloi. The Morlocks, descendants of the working class, lived underground and ate Eloi, a gentle, helpless race descended from the rich.

2. Vivisection—surgery and experimentation on live animals. In Wells's day, the morality and scientific value of vivisection was a hot topic for debate.

3. Mars. Like many of his creations, Wells's Martian invaders became a cliché of later science fiction writing and films.

4. Because listeners believed that it was a real newscast about a Martian invasion! Howard Koch had adapted Wells's novel to be read as a series of emergency news broadcasts about invading aliens, and the actor Orson Welles's performance alarmed many listeners—more than a million, according to a study by the sociologist Hadley Cantril.

5. Charles Darwin, whose theory of evolution had a heavy influence on Wells's writing. Huxley called himself "Darwin's Bulldog."

DON'T KNOW MUCH ABOUT
Lewis Carroll

Hard to believe, but the author of *Alice's Adventures in Wonderland* had a reputation for being dull and uninspiring at his day job: mathematics lecturer at Oxford University. But when Charles Lutwidge Dodgson (1832–1898), mathematician, took on the pen name "Lewis Carroll," he dreamed up fantastical stories that charmed children and adults alike. Preferring the company of little girls throughout his adult life—a fact that has perplexed and concerned his critics—Dodgson wrote playful nonsense to delight young readers. Among his best-loved works are *Alice's Adventures in Wonderland* (1865) and its sequel, *Through the Looking-Glass, and What Alice Found There* (1871). Are you growing "curiouser and curiouser" about the Wonderland that Carroll created? Then follow Alice down the rabbit hole and take this quick quiz.

1. Was Alice based on a real person?

2. Who says the famous line, "Off with her head!"?

3. Which *Wonderland* character can vanish as he pleases, leaving his grin to disappear last?

4. Which poem, included in *Through the Looking-Glass*, introduced invented words like "brillig," "slithy," "wabe," and "mimsy"?

5. In *Through the Looking-Glass*, what nonsensical poem do Tweedledum and Tweedledee sing?

6. What Woodstock-era rock song used characters and symbols from Carroll's *Alice* books to describe the psychedelic effects of drugs like LSD?

ANSWERS

1. Yes. Though the stories were clearly works of the imagination, their heroine was inspired by Alice Liddell, the daughter of one of Dodgson's Oxford colleagues.

2. The Queen of Hearts—a playing card come to life in *Alice's Adventures*.

3. The Cheshire Cat.

4. "Jabberwocky." Humpty Dumpty explains these foreign words to Alice.

5. "The Walrus and the Carpenter."

6. "White Rabbit," by Jefferson Airplane. The line "Go ask Alice" later became the title of a 1971 book, allegedly the diary of an anonymous teenage drug addict.

DON'T KNOW MUCH ABOUT
Chinua Achebe

"Always use the word 'Africa' or 'Darkness' or 'Safari' in your title," wrote the Kenyan author Binyavanga Wainaina in his tongue-in-cheek 2005 essay, "How to Write About Africa"—poking satirically at the one-note portrayals of Africa and Africans that have long been the norm in Western literature. In the 1950s the Nigerian author Chinua Achebe (b. 1930) set out to change all that. Called the father of modern African literature, Achebe burst onto the literary scene with *Things Fall Apart* (1958). Before that novel, Achebe has said, "The story of our position in the world had been told by others." This quick quiz will test your knowledge of Achebe and his work.

TRUE OR FALSE?

1. Achebe writes his fiction in his first language, Igbo.

2. Achebe is the most translated African writer in the world.

3. The title of *Things Fall Apart* was taken from Shakespeare's *Hamlet*.

4. *Things Fall Apart* takes place during the Nigerian nationalist movement of the 1950s.

ANSWERS

1. False. Achebe writes in English, the language that he was schooled in. He has, however, said, "When I'm writing in English, Igbo is standing next to it."

2. True. *Things Fall Apart* has been translated into more than fifty languages.

3. False. The phrase comes from W. B. Yeats's poem "The Second Coming."

4. False. It is set in the 1890s, during the time when British colonial governors and Christian missionaries were expanding into Igboland, in eastern Nigeria.

DON'T KNOW MUCH ABOUT
Christmas Classics

There's no doubt about it: "The Night Before Christmas" is a classic holiday poem. Just who authored it, however, is a murkier issue. Originally titled "A Visit from St. Nicholas," the poem was published anonymously in a Troy, New York, newspaper in 1823. For years the public believed that Clement Clark Moore, a New York City clergyman and Bible scholar, had written it. Others maintain, however, that the author was the Poughkeepsie-based poet Major Henry Livingston Jr. and that Moore—whose other verses are more somber and less playful—claimed authorship only after Livingston's death. Though the controversy has not yet been put to bed, the poem remains a Christmas Eve bedtime favorite for many children. If visions of sugarplums are already dancing in your head, you'll be able to answer these Christmas literature questions "in a twinkling."

1. Which American writer recalled his older friend exclaiming, "Oh my, it's fruitcake weather!"?

2. In Dr. Seuss's illustrated book *How the Grinch Stole Christmas* (1957), what color is the Grinch?

3. Which Christmas book ends with the immortal line, "God bless us, every one!"?

4. Which Christmas-themed short story, featuring Jim and Della Young, is often cited as an example of irony?

5. How many of the eight reindeer from "The Night Before Christmas" can you name?

ANSWERS

1. Truman Capote, in *A Christmas Memory* (1956).

2. Though he wears a red suit, the Grinch himself is drawn in black and white. The Grinch first turned green in his 1966 animated TV special.

3. *A Christmas Carol* (1843), by Charles Dickens.

4. "The Gift of the Magi" (1906), by O. Henry.

5. Dasher, Dancer, Prancer, Vixen, Cupid, Comet, Donder, Blitzen. The last two reindeer were actually called "Dunder" and "Blixem" in the poem's first printing—Dutch for thunder and lightning—which many have interpreted as evidence that the Dutch-speaking Livingston was in fact the poem's true author.

DON'T KNOW MUCH ABOUT
Dostoyevsky

Faith and doubt. Sin, suffering, and redemption. Light reading it is not, but the work of Fyodor Mikhaylovich Dostoyevsky (1821–1881) grapples with some of the biggest questions out there. His novels— *Crime and Punishment* (1866) and *The Brothers Karamazov* (1879–1880) most famous among them— often end on a note of Christian rebirth, but only after the characters have endured much guilt and anguish. In *Crime and Punishment*, Dostoyevsky portrays the inner turmoil of Raskolnikov, a poor student who murders an elderly pawnbroker and her sister, only to confess to the crime soon after. Dostoyevsky knew punishment: he had spent four years as a political prisoner in a Siberian labor camp. Try this Dostoyevsky quiz—it's no "grand inquisition," but it's a tricky one.

1. During the four years that Dostoyevsky spent in Omsk (the Siberian labor camp), what one book was he allowed to read?

2. What medical condition—which also afflicted the fictional characters Smerdyakov (the bastard son in *The Brothers Karamazov*) and Myshkin (the protagonist of *The Idiot*)—did Dostoyevsky suffer throughout his adult life?

3. Who argued, in a 1928 article called "Dostoevsky and Parricide," that *The Brothers Karamazov* reflects the author's own former desire to kill his father?

4. True or false: The Steve Martin comedy *The Jerk* is based on Dostoyevsky's novel *The Idiot*.

ANSWERS

1. The New Testament.

2. Epilepsy.

3. Sigmund Freud. In this article, Freud also claimed that Dostoyevsky's epilepsy began as a result of the guilt that he felt when his father died, a victim of his serfs, in 1839.

4. False. Steve Martin claims, however, that the novel inspired him to change the name of the film from its working title, *Easy Money*.

DON'T KNOW MUCH ABOUT
J. K. Rowling

Think the saga of Harry Potter is incredible? Then consider the rags-to-riches story of the series' author, J. K. Rowling (b. 1965). Before the overnight success of *Harry Potter and the Philosopher's Stone* (1997; released in the United States in 1998 as *Harry Potter and the Sorcerer's Stone*), Rowling was struggling: a single mother in a cramped Edinburgh apartment, she was penniless and living "on the dole" (the British welfare system). But the world fell in love with the bespectacled boy wizard, and the rest is history. Swept up in Pottermania? Take this Rowling quiz to separate the magic of Harry Potter from the Muggle mumbo jumbo.

TRUE OR FALSE?

1. Behind Steven King and Danielle Steele, Rowling is the third-richest author in the world.

2. Rowling's first book, *Harry Potter and the Philosopher's Stone*, sold more copies in the first twenty-four hours than any other book in history.

3. Rowling said that one day "on a crowded train, the idea for Harry Potter simply fell into my head."

4. The Dementors—dark, soul-sucking creatures in *Harry Potter and the Prisoner of Azkaban* (1999)—were inspired by Rowling's own experiences with depression.

ANSWERS

1. False. Rowling is the richest: according to *Forbes* magazine, she is the world's only billionaire author.

2. False. Although *Philosopher's Stone* was a smash hit, the last installment of the series—*Harry Potter and the Deathly Hallows*—was the fastest-selling book of all time. The day it was released in 2007, more than 11 million copies flew off shelves.

3. True. Delayed for several hours without a pen, Rowling sat while her ideas about Potter "bubbled up." This was in 1990, seven years before the first book was published.

4. True. In interviews, Rowling has spoken about that struggle and the benefits of seeking counseling.

DON'T KNOW MUCH ABOUT
Sir Arthur Conan Doyle

"Heaven knows what the objects of his studies are," Dr. John Watson is warned before meeting Sherlock Holmes in *A Study in Scarlet*, the 1887 novel that introduced readers to the crime-solving legend. Arthur Conan Doyle (1859–1930) created the brilliant detective not realizing that mystery stories—rather than historical novels, serious poems, or plays—would be his ticket to fame. Holmes, who was called "Sheridan Hope" in Doyle's early drafts, would of course become an icon. Through the years, artists' and actors' interpretations have made him an unmistakable figure in a deerstalker cap. Think you're a Sherlock Holmes sleuth? Then solving this quiz should be "elementary."

TRUE OR FALSE?

1. Doyle mischievously signed autographs, "Sherlock Holmes."

2. Like the fictional Dr. John Watson, Arthur Conan Doyle was a medical doctor.

3. Sherlock Holmes and his nemesis Professor Moriarty die in one story, only to reappear in later works.

4. Doyle was a master of *baritsu*, the discipline of Japanese wrestling that helped Holmes defeat Moriarty (as Holmes explains in "The Adventure of the Empty House").

5. Although Sherlock Holmes always uses reason to untangle supposedly supernatural mysteries, Doyle was drawn to the occult.

6. In a "lost manuscript," Holmes is cured of his cocaine addiction by Sigmund Freud.

ANSWERS

1. False. But Doyle did often sign as "Dr. John Watson"—Holmes's close friend and chronicler.

2. True. He gave up his practice to write full-time, but in 1900 he volunteered to be a doctor to British troops in Africa. The experience inspired his nonfiction book *The Great Boer War* (1900).

3. True. Eager to pursue more serious writing, Doyle depicted the apparent deaths of Holmes and Moriarty in "The Adventure of the Final Problem," published in the *Strand* magazine in 1893. Twenty thousand angry fans canceled their subscriptions!

4. False. *Baritsu* was fictional, though it was likely inspired by "bartitsu," a turn-of-the-century British self-defense fad that incorporated walking sticks as weapons.

5. True. In novels like *The Hound of the Baskervilles* (1902), reason triumphed—but mystical matters fascinated Doyle, and in 1926 he published *The History of Spiritualism*.

6. True. Doyle did not write this manuscript, however; *The Seven-Per-Cent-Solution* (1974) was written by Nicholas Meyer.

DON'T KNOW MUCH ABOUT
To Kill a Mockingbird

If you publish only one book, may as well make it a good one. For Harper Lee, it was *To Kill a Mockingbird* (1960), the story of Scout Finch, a girl growing up in a small Southern town. Scout and her brother Jem wake up to the intolerance and racial hatred around them when their father, Atticus, takes on the legal case of a black man accused of raping a white woman. *To Kill a Mockingbird* won the Pulitzer Prize in 1961, and in the last ten years, it has been far and away the most popular selection for "One Book, One Community" reading programs—for example, every Chicago resident was encouraged to read the novel in 2001. Do you know why it's a sin to kill a mockingbird? Take this quick quiz on the beloved coming-of-age novel.

1. In what fictional town is *To Kill a Mockingbird* set?

2. In which real Alabama town were nine black teenagers falsely accused of raping two white women in 1931?

3. Which character in *To Kill a Mockingbird* did Lee base on her childhood friend Truman Capote?

4. What is the name of Scout's reclusive neighbor, whom she begins to understand better at the end of the novel?

5. Who won an Oscar for his role as Atticus Finch in the 1962 film version of the novel?

ANSWERS

1. Maycomb, Alabama.

2. Scottsboro. The case of the "Scottsboro Boys" provided real-life inspiration for Lee's novel.

3. Dill Harris, Scout Finch's friend and neighbor. Lee was the prototype for one of Capote's characters: Idabel Tompkins in *Other Voices, Other Rooms* (1948).

4. Boo Radley.

5. Gregory Peck. Another of Peck's great roles from literature was in the 1956 film *Moby-Dick*; he played Captain Ahab.

DON'T KNOW MUCH ABOUT
Literary Hoaxes

In 2006 the Web site "The Smoking Gun" exposed what it called "a million little lies" in James Frey's bestselling memoir, *A Million Little Pieces*. Then in 2008 Margaret B. Jones's memoir of Los Angeles gang life, *Love and Consequences*, was revealed as a total fake when the sister of the author (whose real name was Margaret Seltzer) came forward. But literary fakes and forgeries are nothing new. See which of these notable literary hoaxes you can sniff out.

1. Whose "authorized autobiography" did Clifford Irving sell for $765,000—without that person's knowledge?

2. Which smutty novel, allegedly by "Penelope Ashe," was actually authored by twenty-five

journalists curious to see whether Americans would buy a tasteless and trashy book?

3. Whose "diaries" did the swindler Konrad Kujau forge and sell to a German magazine for $4.8 million?

4. Which book—allegedly a memoir of the author's Cherokee childhood—was later revealed to be the work of the Ku Klux Klan organizer Asa Earl Carter?

5. Which 1971 book, billed as the "real diary" of a fifteen-year-old drug addict, was later exposed as the work of several adult authors, including the editor Beatrice Sparks?

6. Which 1956 novel caused a stir when a radio personality told listeners to ask for it in stores—though the book and its author did not yet exist?

7. Which alleged memoir, describing a white woman's experience of an Aboriginal Australian "walkabout," elicited public outcry from Aboriginal groups who called the book a hoax?

ANSWERS

1. Howard Hughes, the rich and reclusive aircraft industry tycoon. Once discovered, Irving served jail time for the hoax.

2. *Naked Came the Stranger* (1969), by Mike McGrady and twenty-four others. The book was a bestseller.

3. Adolf Hitler. Kujau's hoax was revealed when authorities discovered postwar ink, paper, and glue in the diaries. He spent three years in prison for the forgery.

4. *The Education of Little Tree* (1976), published under the name "Forrest Carter."

5. *Go Ask Alice.*

6. *I, Libertine,* by Frederick R. Ewing. The radio host Jean "Shep" Shepherd invented the author and title and started a media frenzy. In an ironic twist, Ballantine Books commissioned and published a novel fitting Shepherd's description.

7. *Mutant Message Down Under* (1994), by Marlo Morgan. Morgan apologized to Aboriginal elders, but she wavered about the truthfulness of

her book: at times she admitted it was fictional, but she maintained that it was inspired by real events. The book is now considered a work of fiction.

DON'T KNOW MUCH ABOUT
Rudyard Kipling

Rudyard Kipling (1865–1936) is the author most strongly associated with the British Empire. In fact, he coined the term "white man's burden" in an 1899 poem by that name, encouraging the United States to take up the work of colonizing people he considered "half-devil and half-child." Kipling's popularity as a writer rode the wave of jingoism—the patriotic sensibility that drove British imperial expansion—in the late ninteenth century. These days, Kipling's work is generally considered a product of his times: pro-empire, and sometimes racist. However, Kipling's children's stories, like those collected in *The Jungle Book* (1894) and *Just So Stories* (1902), are perennial favorites. If you know "How the Camel Got His Hump" and "How the Leopard Got His Spots," take this quiz to see what else you know.

1. What film, starring Sean Connery and Michael Caine, was inspired by a short story from Kipling's 1888 collection *The Phantom Rickshaw*?

2. Which famous Kipling character is once referred to as "a man's cub"?

3. What war inspired Kipling's poem "White Man's Burden"?

4. Which *Jungle Book* character was a heroic mongoose?

5. Which Kipling novel told the story of an Irish orphan who becomes the disciple of a Tibetan holy man?

ANSWERS

1. *The Man Who Would Be King* (1975), directed by John Huston.

2. Mowgli, the hero of many stories in *The Jungle Book*.

3. The Spanish-American War (1898), which ended with the United States seizing control of newly liberated lands like Cuba and the Philippines, which had been Spanish colonies—this explains Kipling's reference to "new-caught, sullen people."

4. Rikki-Tikki-Tavi.

5. *Kim* (1901), considered one of the earliest spy novels.

DON'T KNOW MUCH ABOUT
Truman Capote

"Nonfiction novel"—the term may sound like an oxymoron, but that's what Truman Capote called *In Cold Blood* (1966), his book about a pair of killers and a grisly quadruple murder in Kansas. Applying the techniques of good fiction writing to a story that he claimed was "immaculately factual," Capote (1924–1984) changed the face of journalism. In addition, the fame-loving author became one of the first literary celebrities of the television era. With his high-pitched, Southern-accented speech and his delight in scandal, Capote was like no writer that American viewers had seen before. See if you can ice this quiz about the author of *In Cold Blood*.

1. Which writer, having just completed a novel of her own, traveled with Capote to Kansas to help research *In Cold Blood*?

2. Over the course of *In Cold Blood*, does Capote ever use a first-person narrative voice?

3. How many hours of interviews did Capote tape-record for his *In Cold Blood* research?

4. Which Capote novella became a 1961 Hollywood classic?

5. Which catty story, published in a 1975 issue of *Esquire* magazine, sabotaged Capote's relationships with the "ladies who lunch" set?

ANSWERS

1. Harper Lee. According to Capote, Lee was useful not only for her note taking but also because "she became friendly with all the churchgoers."

2. No—not even once. Capote felt that a writer should not intrude in his story.

3. None. Opposed to using tape recorders, Capote took thousands of pages of notes.

4. *Breakfast at Tiffany's* (1958). Holly Golightly was famously portrayed by Audrey Hepburn.

5. "La Côte Basque." The story—actually a chapter from an unfinished novel called *Answered Prayers*—shared the scandals of Capote's high-society friends, in some cases naming names.

DON'T KNOW MUCH ABOUT
Famous Theater Lines

Nothing's more determined than a cat on a hot
in roof—is there? Is there, baby?

Not too hard to figure out that that line comes from the Tennessee Williams play *Cat on a Hot Tin Roof* (1955). But what about these memorable lines from some notable plays? Can you identify the playwright and the play?

1. For every man who lives without freedom, the rest of us must face the guilt.

2. I can resist everything except temptation.

3. Gin was mother's milk to her.

4. I hope that was an empty bottle, George. You don't want to waste good liquor . . . not on your salary.

5. Tell me about the rabbits, George.

6. Oh, the shark has pretty teeth, dear.

7. You see things; and you say, "Why?" But I dream things that never were; and I say, "Why not?"

ANSWERS

1. Lillian Hellman, from *Watch on the Rhine*.

2. Oscar Wilde, from *Lady Windermere's Fan*.

3. George Bernard Shaw, from *Pygmalion*.

4. Edward Albee, from *Who's Afraid of Virginia Woolf*.

5. John Steinbeck, from the stage version of *Of Mice and Men*.

6. Bertolt Brecht, from *The Threepenny Opera*.

7. Often quoted by Robert F. Kennedy and attributed to him, this quotation is actually by George Bernard Shaw, from *Back to Methuselah*.

DON'T KNOW MUCH ABOUT
The Psalms

The world's most popular book of poetry is not by Shakespeare, Dickinson, or Keats. It's the biblical book of Psalms. Martin Luther said that the Psalms were "a Bible in miniature." The 150 poems collected in the Book of Psalms are at the heart of Jewish worship and have influenced Western music, language, and literature for centuries. Even Jesus quoted a Psalm, number 22, when he said, "Why have you forsaken me?" What do you know about the collection of poems that Saint Augustine once called "the language of devotion"?

1. **Who wrote the Psalms?**

2. **What is the most popular Psalm?**

3. Which Psalm is known as the *De profundis*?

4. In Psalm 137, the psalmist asks for a blessing for what grim act?

5. What do the Psalms have to do with rosary beads?

6. Biblical bonus question: Pete Seeger adapted the words and the Byrds made it a hit. But what biblical book inspired the pop classic "Turn, Turn, Turn"?

ANSWERS

1. In ancient tradition, the Psalms were attributed to King David. The text credits David with seventy-four psalms; twelve are credited to his son Solomon. But modern scholars agree that the collection has multiple authors and was written over long periods of time.

2. It is generally agreed that Psalm 23—which begins "The Lord is my shepherd"—is the most familiar and most widely quoted Psalm.

3. Psalm 130, whose first words are, "Out of the depths I cry to you, O Lord." The title *De profundis* has been used by many poets, including Federico García Lorca, Charles-Pierre Baudelaire, and C. S. Lewis. Oscar Wilde also wrote a long letter from prison to his former lover under the title.

4. The famous Psalm 137, which begins with the words "By the rivers of Babylon," ends: "Happy shall they be who take your little ones and dash them against the rock!"

5. The 150 beads of the rosary correspond to the number of Psalms and are traced to a time when monks recited the Psalms each day.

6. The Old Testament Book of Ecclesiastes, chapter 3, which begins: "For everything there is a season, and a time for every matter under heaven."

DON'T KNOW MUCH ABOUT
Children's Classics

In the great green room, there was a
red balloon . . .

S o begins one of everyone's favorite books, *Good-night, Moon.* For most people, literature begins with the singing of nursery rhymes and the telling of fairy tales. Then we move on to children's books. Some classics defy the ages; others become dated and fall by the wayside, only to be replaced by the work of a new generation of imaginative writers and illustrators who provide the magic that ignites and sustains the love for books. Think you remember your childhood favorites? Identify the children's classics summarized in this quick quiz. . . . Just be careful that Mr. McGregor doesn't catch you in the garden, Peter Rabbit.

1. **Max wears his wolf suit and makes mischief.**

2. Jack and Kack go for a walk through Boston with their siblings.

3. Dorothy Kunhardt made magic with a mirror, a cotton ball, and a few other everyday objects.

4. "The sun did not shine" were just five of the 220 total words used by the author.

5. A longtime contributor to *Playboy* wrote, "Once there was a tree . . . and she loved a little boy."

ANSWERS

1. *Where the Wild Things Are*, by Maurice Sendak (1963).

2. *Make Way for Ducklings*, by Robert McCloskey (1941).

3. *Pat the Bunny* (1940).

4. *The Cat in the Hat*, by Dr. Seuss (1957).

5. *The Giving Tree* (1964), by Shel Silverstein, who wrote and drew cartoons for *Playboy* from 1956 until the time of his death in 1999.

DON'T KNOW MUCH ABOUT
Mysteries

For some, it starts with Nancy Drew. For others, the Hardy Boys. Maybe it was even earlier with Encyclopedia Brown. But lots of readers fall in love with mysteries in all their varieties—whodunit, police procedural, hard-boiled, or legal thriller. From "The Murders in the Rue Morgue," Edgar Allan Poe's 1841 tale that is considered by many to be the first detective story—yes, that's why the mystery writer's award is called an "Edgar"!—through Conan Doyle and Christie to the bestsellers of Patterson, Grisham, or Thomas Harris, mysteries keep us turning pages. Solve the tangled enigma of this quick quiz.

1. **Born Sam—also the name of his most famous creation—he was a veteran of both world**

wars, had a long and stormy relationship with the playwright Lillian Hellman, and was jailed and blacklisted during the McCarthy era.

2. A former policeman, his familiarity with cops was displayed in his first novel, *The New Centurions* (1970), as well as in a famous work of nonfiction about policemen.

3. A descendant of Harriet Beecher Stowe (the author of Uncle Tom's Cabin), she was a reporter who took a job with Virginia's chief medical examiner. Good career move!

4. Born in Belgium and one of the most prolific writers of the twentieth century, he published his first novel in 1919, at age sixteen, but introduced his most famous character in 1930.

ANSWERS

1. Samuel Dashiell Hammett (1894–1961), dean of hard-boiled fiction and creator of Sam Spade, the iconic private eye in *The Maltese Falcon* (1930), as well as Nick and Nora Charles, the hard-drinking, bantering couple created in *The Thin Man* (1934).

2. Joseph Wambaugh (b. 1937), a former LAPD detective, whose many other novels include *The Choirboys* (1975), named one of the Top 100 Crime Novels by the Mystery Writers of America in 1995. His nonfiction includes *The Onion Field* (1973), an account of the sensational kidnapping-murder of a California policeman and the emotional toll that it took on his partner.

3. Patricia Cornwell (b. 1956), whose bestsellers feature the medical examiner Dr. Kay Scarpetta.

4. Georges Simenon (1903–1989), whose Inspector Maigret (Le Commissaire Maigret) first appeared in a 1930 story and was featured in more than one hundred novels and short stories.

DON'T KNOW MUCH ABOUT
Aleksandr Solzhenitsyn

Among the first novels that changed history is *One Day in the Life of Ivan Denisovich*. First appearing in a Soviet journal in 1962, it put the name of Aleksandr Solzhenitsyn (1918–2008) on the map and helped change the course of Soviet Communism. Evoking comparisons with the novels of such Russian giants as Tolstoy and Dostoyevsky, the book spread its author's fame, but soon he was in trouble with Soviet authorities, who began to keep his work from print. In spite of that, Solzhenitsyn was awarded the Nobel Prize in 1970. In half a century, more than 30 million copies of his books, translated into some forty languages, were sold worldwide. Exiled from Soviet society, he later returned to Russia and outlived the Communist regime by nearly two decades. What do you know about this Russian literary giant?

TRUE OR FALSE?

1. Solzhenitsyn was first imprisoned for "disrespecting" Stalin.

2. Composed in prison with no paper, *Ivan Denisovich* was later written from memory.

3. Solzhenitsyn refused his Nobel Prize because he objected to Western immorality.

4. Although known primarily as a novelist, Solzhenitsyn's most important book was a work of history.

5. During a period of enforced exile from Russia, Solzhenitsyn lived in rural Vermont.

ANSWERS

1. True. In a wartime letter he called Stalin "the man with the mustache," earning himself a sentence of eight years in a labor camp.

2. True. Using rosary beads fashioned from chewed bread, he memorized passages until he was later able to record them.

3. False. Solzhenitsyn refused to travel to Stockholm because he feared that the Soviet authorities would not allow him ever to return.

4. True. *The Gulag Archipelago* (1973) is a monumental account of the Soviet labor-camp system, a chain of prisons that held as many as 60 million people during the twentieth century. The book's publication led to Solzhenitsyn's deportation.

5. True. He lived for eighteen years in Cavendish, Vermont, where his neighbors protected his privacy with a sign reading, "No Directions to the Solzhenitsyns."

DON'T KNOW MUCH ABOUT
Last Lines

"It was all a dream . . . or was it?" Luckily, most of our favorite novels have better last lines than that. How many of these famous endings can you identify?

1. **I lingered round them, under that benign sky: watched the moths fluttering among the heath and harebells, listened to the soft wind breathing through the grass, and wondered how any one could ever imagine unquiet slumbers for the sleepers in that quiet earth.**

2. **So we beat on, boats against the current, borne back ceaselessly into the past.**

3. **The creatures outside looked from pig to man, and from man to pig, and from pig to man**

again; but already it was impossible to say which was which.

4. The old man was dreaming about the lions.

5. And it was like a confirmation of their new dreams and excellent intentions that at the end of their journey their daughter sprung to her feet first and stretched her young body.

6. "P.S. please if you get a chanse put some flowrs on Algernons grave in the bak yard."

7. ". . . and yes I said yes I will Yes."

ANSWERS

1. *Wuthering Heights,* by Emily Brontë.

2. *The Great Gatsby,* by F. Scott Fitzgerald.

3. *Animal Farm,* by George Orwell.

4. *The Old Man and the Sea,* by Ernest Hemingway.

5. *The Metamorphosis,* by Franz Kafka.

6. *Flowers for Algernon,* by Daniel Keyes.

7. *Ulysses,* by James Joyce.

Acknowledgments

There are a great many people behind this book besides the authors. I wish to first thank the great team at Harper who made this book a reality. I am grateful to Carrie Kania, Jen Hart, Hope Innelli, Cal Morgan, Andrea Rosen, Alberto Rojas, Diane Burrowes, Virginia Stanley, Nicole Reardon, Laura Reynolds, Emily Walters, and a special word of gratitude to Michael Signorelli.

All of the people at the David Black Literary Agency have also been stalwart supporters, and I am always grateful for the friendship and support of David Black, Leigh Ann Eliseo, Dave Larabell, Gary Morris, Susan Raihofer, Joy Tutela, and Antonella Iannarino.

To the teachers and librarians who gave me a love for books and reading, I am ever grateful. And finally, my greatest thanks always go to my family: my son, Colin, and my wife, Joann. And, of course, my wonderful collaborator, Jenny Davis.

KENNETH C. DAVIS

I would like to thank my high school teachers, especially John Palmer, Karen McConnell, and Joel Thomas-Adams, for introducing me to so many wonderful books and ideas.

JENNY DAVIS

Index of Quizzes

HARPER LUXE

THE NEW LUXURY IN READING

We hope you enjoyed reading
our new, comfortable print size and found it
an experience you would like to repeat.

Well – you're in luck!

HarperLuxe offers the finest in fiction and
nonfiction books in this same larger print size and
paperback format. Light and easy to read, HarperLuxe
paperbacks are for book lovers who want to see
what they are reading without the strain.

For a full listing of titles and
new releases to come, please visit our website:

www.HarperLuxe.com

SEEING IS BELIEVING!